The Honeymoon Is Over

Shirley and Pat Boone

"It does hurt to admit your mistakes and to share some of your most intimate moments as a family with people you don't even know," says Shirley Boone.

Yet in *The Honeymoon Is Over* this is exactly what Shirley and Pat Boone, long-time Hollywood entertainers, have done.

To many readers the Boone family is considered among the "beautiful people" in the entertainment world— free from discouragement, pain or trouble.

But that's not the way the Boones picture it.

As a result of their spiritual renaissance in the early 1970s, they were disfellowshipped by their home church . . . . Heavy financial losses—not one but a number—have plagued them. . . . Ill health in the family has been a continuing problem . . . And just at the time when Shirley and Pat were doing their best to witness to their faith in Jesus Christ in the entertainment world, bitter criticism came from church leaders.

How did Shirley and Pat face such pressures?

How did they handle the rebellious streaks in their four teenage daughters?

How did they determine God's will regarding remaining in the entertain-

(Continued on back flap.)

The Honeymoon Is Over

Shirley and Pat Boone

CREATION HOUSE
CAROL STREAM, ILLINOIS

Published by Creation House, 499 Gundersen Drive,
Carol Stream, Illinois, 60187
Distributed in Canada: Beacon Distributing Ltd.,
104 Consumers Drive, Whitby, Ontario L1N 5T3
Distributed in Australia: Oracle Australia, Ltd.,
18-26 Canterbury Road, Heathmont, Victoria 135

Biblical quotations from the New American Standard Bible
© 1971 are used with permission from the Lockman Foundation.

Verses marked TLB are taken from The Living Bible, copyright 1971
by Tyndale House Publishers, Wheaton, Illinois. Used by permission.

ISBN 0-88419-130-3
Library of Congress Catalog Card No. 77-075818
Printed in the United States of America

Contents

Publisher's Note

Pat and Shirley Boone are a phenomenon in the entertainment world. They have been performing literally since childhood: Shirley began at age six with her father, country/Western singer Red Foley; Pat at age ten as a theater soloist. And they are still at it today in their forties—both with their four daughters and on their own. Moreover, they were married at nineteen and have lived together ever since.

Even more astonishing is the fact that in the gross materialism, sexual permissiveness, alcoholism and drug addiction characterizing their profession, the Boones have consistently identified themselves as Christians and maintained an active church relationship for themselves and their family.

Trouble, however, did come. In the 1960s electronic rock began to crowd out Pat Boone's style of singing, and the "nice boy next door" image he portrayed in his films, faded.

With his career foundering Pat tried to change the image. He allowed himself to be cast in swashbuckling roles which called for drinking and sexual promiscuity. The effort to regain his popularity proved in vain. The films failed.

The effort to restyle his professional image led Pat into a deeper problem. He discovered that his interest in studying the Bible—especially in applying its truths to everyday living—was waning. At the same time his wife Shirley, who had looked to him for spiritual guidance from their early days, now found her husband wandering away from both his home and his faith.

At first, Shirley reacted defensively. Then, in a desperate effort to save the crumbling marriage, she determined to go along—to the theater and cocktail parties and on the gambling sprees.

But all efforts of both Pat and Shirley to find themselves in their rapidly deteriorating world failed miserably. Now—in addition to the ailing career and the troubled marriage—came staggering financial failures.

Was there no end to the Boones' problems? If so, both began to despair of ever seeing it.

Then came the traumatic experience which rocked all of Hollywood. Even the evangelical Christian world was shaken. . . and today—perhaps more than ever—the impact of the Boones' personal witness to their faith in Christ—aired over the national media—may have a greater effect on the secular world than that of any other single family.

The remarkable account of what happened in both of their lives appears in their two books: *A New Song,* by Pat in 1970, and *One Woman's Liberation,* by Shirley in 1972. The amazing success of these books—total sales of more than two and a half million copies and still selling at the rate of more than 100,000 a year—attests to the popularity of this family of professional entertainers.

Now in *The Honeymoon is Over* Pat and Shirley Boone bring the reader up-to-date on what has been happening in the turbulent years between then and now.

More problems? Yes, plenty of them. Frustrations and headaches too.

But for a sheer, gutsy treatment of family life, its trials and joys in our day—and for the triumphant reality of life in fellowship with the Holy Spirit through faith in Christ—this book comes as a bright and shining light to those looking for help and hope.

The Publisher

Preface

They say a singer is only as good as his last record. An actor is as good as his last role. A writer as good as his last script.

If a man is successful, he faces the temptation—and the challenge—of trying to duplicate his success. In this book Shirley and I are resisting that temptation and ignoring that challenge. This is not a sequel to anything, except in the sense that it covers the latest chapters of our lives.

It's been seven years since I wrote anything autobiographical, and it's been almost five years for Shirley. We're not trying to write *One Man's Family* in eight volumes so we thought we were through telling our story.

But we were wrong.

The Bible says that a Christian's life is a "living letter, written by the Holy Spirit." It may well be that the experiences we've had in these last few years, and the principles we've been learning through them, are more urgently important than anything we've shared before. They've been happy years, but heavy with turbulence, change and confrontation.

This book isn't meant to be light, entertaining reading. If you're involved in the family game, chances are you've discovered it's a serious business. At its best, it's fun and fulfilling and wonderful.

But it is not automatic. I'm sure you've found that out

already. In fact, these days the family is an endangered institution.

So Shirley and I hope that sharing our saga will be a blessing, perhaps some kind of help to you. The prizes are well worth the struggle.

Learn a lesson from the butterfly. One day a friend of ours saw one, shuddering on the sidewalk, locked in a seemingly hopeless struggle to free itself from its now-useless cocoon. Feeling pity, he took a pocket knife, carefully cut away the cocoon, and set the butterfly free. To his dismay, it lay on the sidewalk, convulsed weakly for a while, and died.

A biologist told him later, "That was the worst thing you could have done! A butterfly needs that struggle to develop the muscles to fly. By robbing him of the struggle, you made him too weak to live."

This book is the story of some of our hardest struggles and subsequent flight. We dedicate this to butterflies everywhere. We love you . . . .

Shirley and *Pat*

P.S. Our thanks go to Bob Walker, our publisher, for caring and praying and working with us in the exercise of putting this book together.

1
You Got Problems?
Good!

PAT

A knock came at the door of our home in Beverly Hills in the middle of a busy day. A long-time friend had come to ask Shirley some pointed questions.

"I just finished reading Pat's book, *A New Song,* and I get the feeling that all of your problems are over. Could that possibly be true?"

Shirley threw back her head and laughed. "Would you like to know this week's collection?" she asked.

Without going into details, she gave him a partial list of the serious tests we were facing right then. One of our daughters had come down suddenly with a serious illness. Our beloved ninety-two-year-old Papa Foley, Red's dad, had just died. A terribly misleading report had seared across the wire services, spilling onto TV, newspapers and entertainment-world magazines—saying that I was declaring personal bankruptcy! That was only *one* week: the next could have been similar.

"But how can you look and act so happy if you still have all these problems?" Our friend seemed really bewildered.

"That's the difference Jesus makes," Shirley said. "We still have problems, all kinds of problems, and sometimes they seem even bigger than before. Everyone is going to have problems, as long as he lives! But the presence and the power of God's Spirit with*in* us is greater than any of the pressures from *without.*"

That's what this book is about: problems. And principles—and promises.

Not long ago Merv Griffin, whose talk show is one of the most successful on TV today, asked us to take part in one of his "theme shows," to discuss marriage and the family. For twenty minutes or so, we shared with his audience some of our experiences and some of the joy we were discovering as we made the Bible our "marriage manual." Merv was polite and interested, and then brought on a young singer-actress whose views were vastly different. She was living with a man, quite openly. They had a daughter, and saw no need for either a wedding or any kind of bow to convention.

She turned to Shirley and said, quite tolerantly, "What you and Pat have is fine—for you. But for most people today, that just won't work."

Shirley asked softly, "Have you tried it?"

For just a second the young singer seemed flustered, then with a note of defiance, she responded, "No I haven't. I cannot believe that a book written two thousand years ago can tell me how to live today!"

Then my turn came.

"Just because something is old doesn't mean it doesn't work," I said. "The law of gravity, for instance. It's older than the Bible, and it still works. Every time. And it comes from the same Source as the Bible!"

Well, the conversation went in a different direction after that, but the last I heard, the young woman and her mate have parted. She still has the daughter who wears only her mother's name, and the tragic wake of defiance (and ignorance) of God's principles widens behind her.

That's why we want to think with you about *principles*—and promises. Nobody likes commandments, but if you discover that the Creator has provided definite and practical guidelines, *principles for successful living,* and that He backs them up with magnificent promises—even a money-back *guarantee* —*and* that He'll look over your shoulder and help you solve the problems, it can be a whole brand new ball game!

I'm talking about real things, the problems of life, liberty, and the pursuit of happiness—in an alien world. I use the word *alien* because I've discovered that society and the world at large are pretty antagonistic to the set of principles Jesus wants us to live by. They crucified Him, didn't they?

There's never been a more loving, giving, unselfish person in all history than the Carpenter from Nazareth. Even non-believers in His origin and divinity admit that He was one swell guy, a wonderful example, a "great teacher." But He didn't fit in; He was definitely an irritant, a misfit—and so they killed Him.

And He wants us to do it *His* way. Follow *Him.*

But if it didn't work for Him, how can it work for us?

It did work for Him. He was doomed from the minute He was born, and He came to know that, even as a child. He understood that He was living in an enemy camp, that He was destined for martyrdom, that He was living under a death sentence. And you know something?

So are you.

We all are. There's only one way to get out of this world *alive—His* way! He made it! He actually lived and loved and laughed and made the deepest footprints ever made on this planet, actually changing its history and its destiny, without making one mistake. He infiltrated the enemy camp, captured the flag, and got home free!

He's got the map, and nobody else does. It's called the Bible.

Now, please don't turn me off, not just yet. This book is not a preachment, a holy "how-to" book; it's an honest sharing of two people's lives, our very common problems, and the *prin-*

ciples that we've discovered in the Manufacturer's Handbook.
Jesus showed us how it is *supposed* to work! Right after
He was baptized by John the Baptist in the Jordan River,
immediately after God spoke audibly from heaven, "This is My
beloved Son, in whom I'm well pleased," right after Jesus
received a special manifestation of the Holy Spirit in the form
of a descending dove—God led His own Son *out into the
wilderness* to be tempted by the devil himself!

Sounds extremely harsh, and blunt, and uncaring, doesn't it?
Almost like the parents we've heard of who've taught their kids
to swim by tossing them into the deep water while they were
just little babies.

But Jesus was no little baby. He'd spent most of His thirty
years learning His Father's Word, studying the principles,
testing and trying them—and He was ready now for His final
exam. The devil watched and circled Jesus fasting out there in
the desert, biding his time. He waited for just the right moment
to pounce on this "defenseless," weakened, innocent victim. He
knew full well that Jesus' birth, childhood and lineage all
pointed to Him as the promised Messiah of Israel, that His very
name indicated He would save the people of Israel from their
sins. He had to take his best shots; he *had* to prevail over this
second Adam, just as he had the first one.

He struck out—and completely! He took three swings,
using all his considerable craft and skill, and never came close.
Why? *Jesus knew and used the principles!*

Whenever I've baptized folks, especially entertainment in-
dustry people, in our swimming pool (or anywhere else), I've
read them this story and warned them to brace themselves, to
get hungrily into God's Word. The devil still works the same
way, and will be circling them just like he did Jesus. The
honeymoon may not last long.

"After I became a Christian, it seemed like my life went to
pieces, everything went wrong!"

I've heard this so many times from actors and directors,
from people in many walks of life, and I know what they're

talking about. We have had the same experience.

"Congratulations!" I usually say. "God's paid you a great compliment! He's treating you like He did His own Son!"

I often remind them of Joseph in the last part of the Genesis account in the Bible. How he was sold into slavery by his own brothers, how he was falsely accused by the wife of the man he'd served so faithfully, and put in prison to die. For years he'd tried to be the kind of man God wanted him to be, and for years he'd been sold and slandered and enslaved. I marvel at his faith, but I suspect he sensed that God was with him, teaching him principles that some day he'd put into practice with more visible results.

And he was right! Before his life came to an end, he was the second most powerful man in the Egyptian empire, the savior of his own brethren, and one of the spiritual giants of all time! *Because he learned and practiced the principles!*

I don't want to scare you; I really don't, but this book comes with a serious warning. If you're a believer in God and the Bible, if Jesus has saved and cleansed you, and especially if you've been baptized and filled with His Holy Spirit—look out! The devil is circling and waiting, and perhaps has already begun an all-out attack on you, your family and loved ones, your business, your ambitions, your health, and may even be tempting you to take your life, just as he did Jesus.

I'm seeing it all the time. It happened to one of my close friends. Right after he really committed his life to the Lord and had a terrific period of spiritual growth and productivity, while his business was prospering and he was finding many opportunities to lead people to Jesus in his office day after day, he confided to me that he was experiencing a strong and mysterious urge *to kill himself!*

"Why, Pat? I've got everything to live for. I'm happily married. I love Jesus and introduce people to Him almost every day. My business is flourishing. Why should I have this terrible urge to take out a gun and shoot myself?"

"Bob," I answered, "you should be honored. Satan is

coming at you with one of his major weapons, one of the carefully honed stilettos he attempted to use on the Son of God Himself! He tried to get Jesus to cast Himself down from a high place—to take His life in His own hands—to "prove" that God wouldn't allow Him to die. He tries this same tactic on selected believers today, too, when he can't get at them some other way. And tragically, he's been successful with a couple of my own friends in the recent past, believers with everything to live for!"

Right then in his office, we prayed and rebuked Satan, and used God's Word just as Jesus did. Bob tells me he's been totally free of that temptation ever since.

That's why Shirley and I believe this book is so important. We ourselves have continued to have lots of problems, lots of challenges, lots of tests and trials in our marriage, our family life, our profession.

Oh, sure . . . there was a wonderful "honeymoon" period for us after our total commitments were made to the Lord and we were filled with His Spirit. The love we experienced was sweeter and more fulfilling than ever before. Whole new dimensions of joy and ability and faith and service opened up to us, and our delight in each other was only exceeded by our delight in the Lord Himself!

Sounds great, doesn't it?

It was—and still is. And getting better.

But, as Bible teacher Bob Mumford has pointed out many times, "The surest evidence of being filled with the Holy Spirit—is trouble!"

That may *not* sound so great, but you've got only two choices. Either take your licks, all the treacherous blows that life and the devil will surely deal you, including eternal separation from God, all by yourself—or allow God to enroll you in His school, fill you with His Spirit, start giving you your daily assignments with some Heavenly homework, and know the incredible peace that comes from knowing He's in the problem *with* you, working in and through you to accomplish

His purpose and make you an overcomer! Take your pick.

In any marriage, there's a period of "newness," of tenderness and patience and happy exploration. But after the "new" wears off, and the problems set in, a man and a woman have to commit themselves to the life-long process of building a *relationship*. Shirley and I have learned some principles about that, and we want to share them with you.

But every believer has a honeymoon experience with Jesus, too. Then comes the "crunch," the crisis, the day-by-day challenge to build a solid eternal relationship with the Bridegroom, the Son of God. And He's so wonderful, so dependable, so consistent, so merciful. Still He loves us so much that He demands that we change, grow, stretch and blossom, that we become more like Him!

And it's not easy. It takes problems, and principles, and promises. Shirley and I are learning, and we want to show you some of our "homework." We got low grades on some of it, but you might even profit from knowing that!

For us, the honeymoon is over, but the marriage has just begun.

2
Castaways

SHIRLEY

What's the biggest disappointment you've ever experienced?

I don't mean seeing smoke pouring from the oven just before your dinner guests arrive, or hearing some atrocious rumor about you or your family floating back at you through a friend. We've all had disappointments like that, but usually the situation may partly have been our own fault.

No, I'm asking what problem came as an overwhelming shock to you because you had no control over it? You may even have sensed it coming but did not believe that it would actually happen until it did—and then you wondered, "But how could anybody ever do this to me?"

Well, if you've read Pat's and my books, you know that some mighty big things happened in our lives a few years ago. Yes, we had been considered among the "nice people" of Hollywood. We had been married for fifteen years, which by Hollywood standards is most unusual. In addition, we had four daughters who were just coming into their teenage years, and they were causing us no serious trouble. Also, we were regular church members, which may have been most remarkable of all.

What people didn't know, however, was that we were in deep trouble. Beginning early in his career Pat had made more than a dozen gold records, headed up his own TV show and played the lead in a number of films which had lifted him into the "top ten" at the box office.

Then the Hollywood mood changed. Now producers were looking for the blood-and-guts type of character, the rebel, the "non-hero." Sex and more sex was the theme of the day. No matter how hard his agent worked, movies that Pat could or would make were almost nonexistent.

But Pat had a growing family and many other responsibilities. He was still a young man with the usual ambitions and career goals, and he wanted to maintain his position in the entertainment business. So he attempted to change his image. He played the lead part in several films which really bothered me, because they were obviously compromises with his earlier convictions. I was almost glad to see them fail.

But also I could see that something was happening to Pat. Because I wasn't interested in going to Hollywood parties, in appearing at all the "right" functions, we drew further and further apart. He accepted engagements in Las Vegas, and I knew he was gambling and starting to drink. Sometimes I could smell alcohol on his breath. In desperation I pleaded with him.

"Pat, please sit down with me and let's decide where we're headed," I would say.

"Everything will work out all right," he would reply. "We're Christians, we go to church regularly. But we've just got to loosen up some, learn to 'fit in' a little."

Finally, more to save our crumbling relationship than for any other reason, I said to myself, "Okay. I love my four girls and I love Pat. If the only way I can keep my family together is to go along with him, that's what I'll do."

The results were anything but good. Pat became concerned. He saw me having an occasional drink and enjoying the attentions of other men. Now *both* of us were miserable.

I was sure Pat didn't love me. And by that time I didn't think

God did either. I couldn't blame God for not loving me, but Pat—oh, how I still wanted him. The longing came somewhat from wounded pride, although I didn't realize it for awhile. The point was, now everything was gone. My marriage, my faith, all that I valued.

Previously, when I feared I was losing Pat, I could turn to God and thank Him for being with me though everyone else had turned away. But approaching my deepest agony, I felt that my Lord, as well as my husband, had rejected me. I couldn't blame them anymore, because I was so aware of my own failings.

Some nights when Pat was away from home, I'd go down into the den and fall on my knees, sobbing. Sometimes I'd literally cry out into the lonely silence, "Jesus, please be with me! Do something. Help me!"

And Jesus heard, though I didn't think so at the time. Through the suffering, He was whispering to me, "Shirley, you're on the wrong track. Quit struggling—come to me my way."

Kneeling, weeping, hopeless, I thought I was losing my mind.

Then it happened. God, through His Holy Spirit, revealed to both Pat and me Jesus' power to work miracles in our day—the miracle of restoration of ourselves to Him, of an inner healing of mind and heart, and of many other demonstrations of His might and power to overcome our physical limitations. It began for both of us with what the Bible describes as the baptism in the Holy Spirit.

The deep and moving reality of that experience and the exciting days that immediately followed, we both have already recorded, so I'll not take time here to repeat. In fact, the purpose of this book is to share with you the experiences that have followed *since,* now that those honeymoon days are over.

"—and they lived happily ever after. The End."

What young girl hasn't looked forward to that in her life? I surely did; I really *expected* it! But I've finally learned that if your goal in life is just to be happy, you'll never achieve it. True happiness—deep, real and lasting happiness—can only come from knowing who God wants you to be, what He expects of your life, and a real sense of His loving guidance from day to day.

What you and I both want is to live happily ever after—right *now!* Isn't it? Well, Pat and I hope that by sharing with you some of the trauma and triumph in our recent lives together, we can help you make the same discovery we've made, only quicker: that honest-to-goodness, right-now happiness can only come from real commitment to the loving Creator God, Who is just as interested in our right-now as we are!

As Pat has already suggested, life is full of problems. They come to all of us, and we really shouldn't be surprised when they do. In fact (although I realize this is difficult), we should thank the Lord for them. It is through them that we come to know Him better and learn how to rely more completely upon Him.

Yes, we were caught up in the euphoria of our new-found faith in God, in His reality, in His power and the presence of His Holy Spirit. But very soon, right in the midst of this happiness, terrific setbacks rocked us—"homework assignments" that would teach us important lessons.

Ah, yes! The first—and perhaps the most devastating—came as a bewildering disappointment. And like many disappointments, it came from an almost unexpected quarter—our own church, the bustling Inglewood congregation where we'd been active members for ten years.

No sooner had we begun to share with our friends and Pat had written his book, *A New Song,* than we began to run into deep doctrinal conflicts with the elders of the church. Pat himself was a deacon there, a song leader and once in a while they'd ask him to preach. When he spoke it was only natural that he should tell about the miracles we'd experienced, the people we knew who were meeting Jesus, and who more often than not were being baptized in our swimming pool.

The elders approved the conversions and the baptisms. But when he also told about praying for someone and seeing that person miraculously healed of an illness, or that we were seeing and experiencing the gifts of the Holy Spirit in action, they objected.

"We believe the Bible is God's book and it provides us with the instructions we need to lead a successful Christian life," they said. "But don't expect to see miracles happen today as they did in Bible times. That day is past."

As a result, Pat was called to frequent meetings with the elders. In fact, it got so that he was at these meetings almost every Sunday afternoon while the girls and I stayed home.

"What you are saying is all good," they would begin, "but don't use the word *miracle,* and don't get carried away in your enthusiasm. You might give our people the impression that God is actually performing miracles or doing supernatural things today. We simply don't want to give this false impression."

Of course, we knew what they were talking about, because we both had been thoroughly steeped in our church doctrine. Pat had grown up in this church fellowship, had studied and taught its doctrine, and had even preached for a small congregation in Texas after we were first married. And we *wanted* to be corrected, if we were wrong somehow. But we also were well aware of what God was showing us through His Word. The day of miracles was *not* over. The Scriptures plainly said that Jesus Christ "is the same yesterday, today and forever" (Hebrews 13:8).

So Pat took the opportunity of these meetings to share the good things that had been happening to us—as well as to listen. And he was telling them he believed Christians had been settling for far less than what God had wanted them to have, because of a limited doctrinal viewpoint.

But the elders were certain we were "misled." After many months of meetings one elder took Pat aside. "Now Pat," he said, "you know we are glad to see this joy, this commitment, this love which you and Shirley have for one another and the Lord. That's wonderful, and we don't want to take it from you . . . if it just wasn't wrapped up with this Holy Spirit bit."

This attitude really shook Pat. It also struck him as sort of funny.

"You know, brother, what you are saying is that you like the *fruit* of the Spirit, and you want us to keep the fruit, but you also want us to get that ugly *tree* out of our yard! The things that you have been seeing in our lives are what Paul calls the fruit of the Holy Spirit in Galatians 5:20. Brother, if we are going to have the fruit we must give the Holy Spirit freedom to work and grow in us. That's what's been happening with Shirley and the girls and me."

By this time a group of elders had gathered around, and another spoke up.

"You know, Pat, every time we talk to you, you want to tell us about some *experience* you've had. You don't believe in the all-sufficiency of the Scripture."

"Brethren, you don't either," Pat replied. "We teach a lot about baptism, quote all the Scriptures on it. Most of our sermons conclude with an invitation to be baptized. Yet we know that until somebody *experiences* baptism that our teaching is in vain. The same goes for praying, singing and giving financially. We preach about them. We teach about them. We believe in them. But at some point they must be *experienced.* So with the Scripture itself—the teaching of it is not sufficient. We must *act* upon it."

To this some of the elders objected. "We're not talking about the same thing."

"But that's what you're saying—that certain Scriptures don't apply to life today. But what I am telling you is that they do. And the reason I know they do is because we have actually experienced them. Like the blind man in John 9 who says, 'I don't know what your doctrine is, but I do know that I was blind *and now I see.'* We too once thought these Scriptures weren't practical any more, but Shirley and I have found that they are. They *do* work. The promises hold true right now!"

We didn't want to cause a division in the church, so as we talked about it, it seemed to Pat and me that we should quietly slip away and go somewhere else. We suggested that—but no, that was not what they wanted. They were our friends and they wanted to be kind to us, but they felt they had to make some public decision anyway.

It was a tough time, for them and for us. We all did a lot of praying.

Right while all this was going on, Dean Dennis, a brilliant young minister who headed up one of our largest congregations in the Los Angeles area, came to visit us. He was a knowledgeable theologian and a most effective speaker. I had a strong hunch that Dean considered me to be the erring one, and was hoping he could influence me "to see the light." If he could straighten me out, surely he could reach the rest of the family and get us back into line.

Dean and his wife Joyce called to ask if they could come and visit with me on Saturday afternoon when Pat was out of town.

I was preparing a chili dinner when they arrived but went into the den and sat down with them. I had been praying that the Lord would give me the words to say, because I was a little bit leary about the confrontation. I loved Dean and Joyce, but after all, he was a preacher and Bible scholar, and I was just a housewife. What could I tell him, how could I argue Scripture with him? Obviously, all I could do was to share with them, honestly and directly, what had *happened* to me and my family.

So despite Dean's bulging briefcase beside him on the chair, which I was sure was loaded with books on church doctrine, I began to tell him how much Jesus meant to me.

"I know why you're here, and I'm not able to argue doctrinal things with you, but nothing you say can alter what has happened to me. I cannot deny the power of the Holy Spirit in my life, ever," I said. And then I told him some of the ways the Lord had miraculously proven His love for me and my family.

To my astonishment—before I had been talking long—he began to weep! (Later, Joyce told me she had never seen Dean cry before in all the time they had been married.) Within a few weeks, the whole Dennis family were baptized in the Holy Spirit!

It certainly wasn't my persuasive power, or my knowledge of the Word of God that brought about this miracle. I believe it was simply the fact that I had told the Lord beforehand that I was not sufficient for the situation. So He took over. It was something like Balaam's talking mule; I was just available.

Shortly after this, the blow fell. One Sunday morning after the church service, one of the elders, a physician and close friend of ours, came up to Pat.

"Tonight we are going to read a document of disfellowshipping. And since you and Shirley are the subjects of it, I wanted to warn you in advance. You probably won't want to be here," he said.

Pat admitted to me later that while he wasn't surprised, the reality of it finally happening stunned him. Immediately he thought of me and how I would take it. So instead of replying to the elder then, he said he would like to talk it over with me and would call him later in the afternoon. On the way home from church we did talk about it, including our daughters in the conversation, and later at home we prayed together. The others didn't say much, but I felt strongly that we all should be present.

To me it was important that the congregation realize that we weren't running off with our tails between our legs. *We* weren't disfellowshipping anybody, though we understood why the elders made their decision. But as far as we were concerned we were all still brothers and we did not believe that we were out of order.

"I believe God will give us grace, so when the document of disfellowshipping is read, the people will see the Holy Spirit in action in us—in our continuing love for them. But if we aren't present they won't see it," I said.

When we called our friend, the elder, he warned Pat, "I want you to know that, as a doctor, I'm worried about Shirley. I believe she's at the point of a nervous breakdown."

Naturally, Pat was puzzled. "What makes you think that?"

"You and I know that Shirley has always been an emotional and somewhat volatile person—she can either be excited and happy or deeply depressed. In the excitement of these spiritual experiences you have been describing to us, she has been exuberant. I've seen that; but I'm afraid this constant "high," this apparent calm, is misleading and has gone way beyond normal. I feel she's like a wire being stretched tighter and tighter and could snap anytime now."

"Well, Doc, I appreciate your concern, but I'm living with her every day, and I'm seeing that she is more able to handle things with a calmness and understanding than she ever was before. I really think you're seeing some of the fruit of the Spirit," Pat replied.

So when the evening service began, the entire family was present. When the time came for the announcement, one of the elders stood up and, with a grave face, apparently struggling to maintain control of his emotions, began to read the statement.

I don't remember all that it said. The idea was that after a year or so of study, the elders had come to the painful conclusion that we had been deluded into some false interpretation of the Scriptures and into thinking that we had experienced miracles today when it was clear that miracles had ceased back in the first century. Therefore, since there was a danger in our influence on other members, they felt it had become necessary to officially and publicly withdraw fellowship from us. They hoped this action would cause us to see the error of our ways, admit it, and again become eligible for membership. They expressed their love for us, and regretted this had become necessary.

The audience sat stunned. Only the elders had known this was coming. Clearly audible gasps sounded across the congregation, and heads turned in our direction.

Up to the time the elder began reading, I had been uneasy. *But the moment he started,* the Lord presented me with a genuine gift of peace, the real sense that we were where we were supposed to be at that moment in time. God gave me a love for the elders, and for the whole congregation, which was absolutely overwhelming. No resentment. No judgment. Literally, the fruit of the Holy Spirit was pouring through me—and I'm sure through Pat and the girls too. We felt an intense love for all of our friends, a deep sense that this was God's will for all of us, and that the letter wasn't the end of anything. It was the beginning of a real adventure with Jesus, who also had been "disfellowshipped." It was a miracle, I think, a real answer to prayer.

"This just can't be," people exclaimed, coming up to us afterwards in tears.

"Please don't leave. You've been such a help and encouragement to us. We need you now more than ever," some said.

Again the Lord gave us peace and reminded us of His own Word.

"Remember that Romans 8:28 says, 'All things work together for good to those who love God.' We love God. The elders love God. Therefore, this must be working together for our good. So let's thank Him for it," we said.

"You know, I don't understand this," said one of the deacons. "We've just disfellowshipped you, and here you are comforting *us!*"

I was right about the incident being just a beginning.

For several years after that Pat received long, long letters from church leaders trying to convince him that we were wrong and had "departed from the faith" and sound doctrine.

Of course, the incident made the news media. Television, *Time* and *Newsweek* magazines and hundreds of newspapers carried the story. We had participated in many big rallies and fund-raising programs sponsored by the leading groups of the fellowship throughout the country. Royalties of more than

$125,000 from Pat's first book, *Twixt Twelve and Twenty* had gone to a church-supported college in Philadelphia. Now he was voted off the board of directors of the college.

The blow on us was heavy. But from it came one of our first lessons in discovering God's sufficiency. We *began to see a principle emerge,* and though we've had to have many "refresher" lessons, the principle has been invaluable to us. It's this: *the Lord is with you.*

Did you know that's one of His names, which He revealed to the children of Israel? Jehovah Shammah, "The Lord is present (Ezekiel 48:35). And didn't Jesus say to all who put their faith in Him, "Behold, *I am with you,* even to the end of the world"?

How could we really learn the comforting truth of that principle if the Lord didn't allow us to go through bleak periods, trials and tests, and disappointments? Only by going through "the valley of the shadow of death" can we really come to know and completely trust the Good Shepherd. When everything else is stripped away, Jesus is there!

Remember His Word, "Thanks be unto God which always causeth us to triumph in Christ and maketh manifest the savour of His knowledge by us *in every place"* (II Corinthians 2:14 KJV).

It was precious to feel the presence of Jesus with us in this "castaway" period. But now, we had no church home. We were a Christian family, and we needed a place where we could get solid Bible instruction for our teenage girls and ourselves. Just as important, we desperately needed the fellowship and encouragement of a loving, caring group of Christians.

. . . And more so, since now lurking in the shadows of the days ahead was an ominous threat to our very survival.

3

It's Only Money

PAT

I guess nothing will get the undivided attention of a man more quickly than money. And if his home, family and life's work are threatened for *lack* of money, everything else fades into the background.

Earning a living is a tricky proposition these days, and building any substantial financial footing for the future seems almost impossible. Housing, food, taxes, clothes, medicine and schooling—all these eat up everything a man can make, and then some! And if he has any hobbies, any dreams for the future, any vacation plans or would-be investment ideas, the pinch is really on.

I think that's why God uses money to teach us lessons. It can be the fastest route, the sharpest way to teach us how completely we can trust Him with everything.

Boy, He gave me a crash course! First $700,000, then $2 million and finally $30 million! I ought to be a graduate by now, a Ph.D., but I'm still learning.

A business partner and I bought the Oakland franchise from the newly formed American Basketball Association. Since I was already up to my ears keeping several TV shows going, recording and doing appearances in various parts of the country and the world, we decided my partner should keep the majority of stock and run the operation. The first year was "El Floppo," a gigantic disaster. We lost a million bucks, but went cheerfully into the next season—and lost another million! In September of 1968, I received a frantic call from my accountant. There had been an incredible overdraft by the Oakland Oaks management, and the bank was demanding $700,000 from *me* within twenty-four hours!

Fortunately, the Wendell West Real Estate Company, of which I was a director, was able to lend me the money. That crisis was averted temporarily, but soon my financial advisers hit me with a double whammy: at the rate the Oakland Oaks had been losing money I was now liable for $2 million. My partner had empty pockets, and, of course, I had the $700,000 loan to pay back—and soon.

Then, through a miraculous set of circumstances, in which my eyes were opened to the reality of the intervention of the Holy Spirit in the affairs of my life, I suddenly found myself at peace—in spite of the growing financial crisis.

Then another miracle.

"The Oakland Oaks are going to go bankrupt immediately," my financial counselors told me. "Then the bank will come against your partner and quickly bankrupt him. Next they will come against you. We believe we have a fighting chance by allowing them to attach everything you've got rather than throwing you into bankruptcy. Everything possible will be sold, and then you will be able to work off the indebtedness in the years to come."

Well, I suppose I should have felt completely zonked. But I didn't.

"Thanks guys, you've done your best," I said. "We appreciate it. But we're completely out of answers, aren't we? Now that we all give up—watch. *God is going to solve this.*"

And He did! Two days later a man by the name of Earl Forman from Washington, D.C. bought the Oakland Oaks for close to $2 million, and flew back East. It was such a breathtaking miracle, such a hallelujah time, that I thought my troubles were over.

Not by a long shot. I was starting to glimpse a principle though. *You can actually trust the Lord with your business.*

Up to this point I had also put my confidence in financial counselors who had far more wisdom than I did. But I soon discovered that no matter how sharp and honest and diligent they might be, situations often develop over which even they have no control.

You see, the Lord had some more problems for me to solve in another financial cave-in that was far worse!

In the spring of 1970 my attorney wanted to clear up one little matter. I had become a general partner in the Wendell West Company, one of the most successful real estate operations of the day. Beginning in the Northwest twelve years before, it had scored a string of unbroken successes. By that time it had thirty offices in various parts of the country and had even begun purchasing and developing land outside of the U.S. Although I was not involved in management decisions, because of my visibility as an entertainer, I was probably the best-known director of the company. This "visibility" concerned my attorney.

"This is a fast-growing company," he said, "and while it's been successful so far, by the very nature of its activity, it must borrow huge sums of money to finance future growth. As a full partner in the business you are automatically—although only theoretically—responsible for all of the potential debts of the company."

"What's your recommendation?" I asked.

"We should remove you from this exposure. As a limited partner instead of a general partner, you would not have this liability," he said.

In the end, company officials and I agreed that I would reduce my share of ownership from 10 to 5 percent. They would remove me from the direct liability for loan agreements entered into by the company. As a part of the arrangement, I agreed to spend half of my working time in 1970 representing the company at various public functions throughout the country. And in return for a very lucrative work contract, I would postpone some of my entertaining activities.

We returned from Seattle feeling great. My lawyer was satisfied that I would no longer be liable for Wendell West Company loans. I was satisfied that I was building something solid for the future, and that it was good for all concerned, from the company president to the smallest investor in one of our properties.

Suddenly, the rug was pulled out from under me. Within several months it became apparent the real estate market nationwide was going bust! Remember the big recession of 1970?

First, two big lending institutions withdrew $20 million in financing they had promised the Wendell West Company.

"We've committed this money to you, but we simply don't have it," they admitted. "You'll have to get it from some other source." They were struggling for their *own* financial lives!

Frantically, the officers attempted to find other sources for the $20 million. None were available. Then the company officers began shutting down offices and letting employees go. But all their efforts to stabilize the financial position of the company failed. In the end the company applied for relief under a provision of the federal tax code which allows a company to file for bankruptcy but continue operating for five years without the claims of creditors. This preserves its assets for the stockholders.

Overnight a lopsided news story blared across the wire services: "Pat Boone goes into bankruptcy. Famous entertainer $30 million in debt."

"What next?" I thought. "I've divested myself of my general partnership. I'll receive no compensation for the six months I've worked for the company, and the entertainment contracts

I turned down are gone. Now the Lord allows me to be tabbed as bankrupt."

The communications media in Seattle broke the news first. Next came Los Angeles—with the *Times* and the *Herald Examiner*, as well as all the TV channels. Then we received clippings from the *Nashville Banner*, the *Tennessean* and newspapers in other states. The entertainment trade papers were next—the *Hollywood Reporter*, the *Daily, Variety* and *Billboard*. Finally came the financial press: *Wall Street Journal, Forbes* and *Fortune*. And probably some others that I forget or did not see—all claiming that Pat Boone was bankrupt to the tune of $30 million.

Technically, of course, this wasn't true. I still had some assets—our home—and some other investments. But if the worst ever happened, there was no way I could cover the $30 million liability.

Shirley and I cried out to God.

"What a terrible testimony this is, Lord. We're sorry for making it seem as though a child of Yours has bungled so badly. What can we do?"

In the end I went up to the Wendell West headquarters to meet with the board of directors. Some of them had read *A New Song.*

"If God got you out of the Oakland Oaks situation, ask Him to get us out of this problem," one suggested, almost hopefully.

"Fellas, unless we get on our knees before God, we're not going to find a solution," I said. "This is bigger than we can handle."

At this, one of the partners bristled, "*You* pray. We'll work."

"I *have* worked," I said "and probably I've spent as much time as some of you—and despite the financial guarantee you've made me, I'll get nothing. What's more, my name and reputation of fifteen years as a successful entertainer can go down the drain."

Then I told them that I had been talking to the Lord about the problems of the company, and I was convinced that He was telling us that only by coming to Him could we find the solution.

"I have worked and will continue to work, but I'm just saying that until we get on our knees—each one of us—I don't believe we'll ever get out of this mess we're in," I said.

By now the man who had bristled earlier had cooled off.

"You know, Pat, you may be right," he said. "We all do need to pray . . . and we really need to pull together, if we want to save the company and protect all the people who've believed in us."

Well, the threat of eventual bankruptcy hung over all our heads for the next five years. Finally, in 1975 the court, the Internal Revenue Service and the creditors arrived at a solution. It was a painful one for me.

The agreement called for a final contribution on the part of the company of a half million dollars—and the partners had to come up with it! Although I was no longer a partner, my signature still appeared on some of the early loans, so I was counted "in." But then the attorneys for the creditors told me they expected *me* to put up a major hunk of the half million! This, in spite of the fact that I had made none of the management decisions, had always done what I had been asked to do, and had owned less of the stock than most anybody else in the partnership!

"Look, this isn't fair," I said.

"This has nothing to do with fairness," the other partners replied.

"We don't pretend it's fair. It's just a matter of who has what to give. And since you've got more to give, you'll have to ante up more. Otherwise, it's a wipeout for all of us."

I choked and sputtered and fumed, and almost cried in frustration. It wasn't fair, it was terribly unbalanced, it hurt like crazy—but they were right. There was no other way.

On the other hand, I couldn't forget the day the officers came to my rescue at the time I needed the $700,000 in twenty-four hours to meet the bank's demand on the Oakland Oaks.

They "saved my life" then—so now it was my turn.

And I really believe that the horrible strain of that five-year struggle to come back from bankruptcy had by now brought every one of the partners to his knees. I'll just bet there were many anguished hours before the throne of God for each of us. And who knows?—if this financial disaster hadn't confronted us, some of us might *never* have come to the realization of how much we need God, all the time, every day!

That's what I mean about God using money to teach us lessons. And I'm telling you right now, I've got a whole lot more to learn, as you'll see.

There was a magnificent, simple but powerful principle still trying to emerge through my financial trials, and I hadn't quite grasped it. It's fantastic, and I'll share it with you later—but even now, I was experiencing the truth of Romans 5:3-5, "We can rejoice, too, when we run into problems and trials, for we know that they are good for us—they help us learn to be patient.

"And patience develops strength of character in us and helps us trust God more each time we use it, until finally our hope and faith are strong and steady.

"Then, when that happens, we are able to hold our heads high no matter what happens and know that all is well, for we know how dearly God loves us, and we feel this warm love everywhere within us because God has given us the Holy Spirit to fill our hearts with His love" (TLB).

I discovered that this wasn't just a Bible passage! It was real!

A number of my friends, who knew the financial cloud I was under, told me over and over, "We don't see how you keep going under this strain, knowing any minute the ceiling may fall in. And you have to keep going on TV and personal appearances and all the rest, as if everything were fine—and you don't ever seem worried!"

"Well," I'd usually say, "you know about what's happening on the *out*side of me—let me tell you about what God's doing on the *in*side. It's amazing!"

The Boones learned many lessons about the use of money and material possessions.

4

Jesus vs. Joseph

SHIRLEY & PAT

As we tell this highly sensitive chapter of our lives, we have no desire to hurt or criticize anyone. We've learned some good lessons from our friendship with Mormon people. Almost without exception, they've proven themselves to be honest, industrious, moral and loving. Few groups can match their example of family closeness, devotion to church teaching and its integration into daily living and business practice. They take care of their own, and they're zealous; we treasure their friendship.

So if you're a Mormon, or a member of one of the other groups mentioned in this chapter, please keep in mind that we're telling just what happened to us from our perspective and from our understanding of God's Word. We love you.

Pat: Now that we'd been officially "bounced" by our church, we were bombarded by other churches and denominations. Our friends in the Baptist church invited us to worship with them. The same went for other friends in the Presbyterian and

Episcopal churches. On several occasions Jehovah Witness ministers came to visit, as did the Krishna people. (I'd love to have a picture of that bald, saffron-robed fellow on our doorstep.) We were also approached by some Roman Catholics and Seventh-Day Adventists.

Shirley: But the most persistent were the Mormons.

Pat: That's right. I guess it was only logical, though, because at that time our oldest daughter, Cherry, was dating a Mormon boy two years older than she was. He was a member of a family we'd long known and loved. We hadn't thought much of it at first, because they were only teenagers at the time. But now that we had moved into a deeper understanding of the Word of God and were discovering that this Word is a living reality for today, Shirley began to have doubts about the budding romance.

Shirley: I said, "Pat, we don't know much about the Mormon church. They all seem to be nice people—at least all the ones we've met. Maybe we'd better check into it, find out more about what they really believe."

Pat: The next thing I knew I received an invitation to speak at Brigham Young University! There was to be a combined audience of students and the public in the gymnasium with a closed-circuit TV for the overflow crowd. We were told there might be twenty thousand people there!

Shirley: As it turned out more than twenty-three thousand jammed into the fieldhouse—and when we walked onto the platform, they gave us a standing ovation.

Pat: It was tremendous. I could hardly believe it . . . and I simply shared with those Mormons what we had shared with our own church folks and anybody else who would listen to us—that God had moved into our lives in a new and wonderful dimension. The Scriptures were coming to life for us. We were seeing miracles happening in our lives and in the lives of our friends. In other words, we were simply rejoicing in a new-found relationship to our wonderful Savior and Lord.

Shirley: After Pat finished he asked if there were any questions. And the first one was, "What do you think about Joseph Smith and the Mormon church?"

Pat: Everybody laughed and applauded. I don't know exactly how they thought I would answer, but they seemed to imply, "How about you becoming Mormons?"

I answered as tactfully as I could without committing myself. I said that several platoons of freshly scrubbed young men from the church had visited us and that we were "looking at the Mormon church very carefully." The roof nearly came off the place then!

Shirley: Actually, there were four separate teams that had come to our home, weren't there?

Pat: Yes, there were. So I said that the more we looked into Mormonism, the more suprised we were by what we found.

"For instance," I said, "we seem to agree on everything that Jesus said in the Bible. But we disagree on some of the things that Joseph Smith (their founder) said."

Then I pointed out that "Jesus and His Word unite us, but Joseph Smith seems to *separate* us, because we're not able to accept the things that Joseph Smith said. Some of the things that Joseph Smith said contradict what Jesus said."

(I've since found out that Mormons handle the contradictions by saying the Bible is incorrectly translated.)

Shirley: The audience grew silent, though still polite and smiling. They seemed to be saying this time, "You keep searching and God will show it to you."

Pat: Well, that really stirred things up! After we returned from Salt Lake City, we were visited by more teams from the Mormon church. We wound up going to the Mormon Temple here in Los Angeles just as we had gone to the temple in Salt Lake City. We met Joseph Fielding Smith, then president of the LDS church, and visited with him and his wife in their apartment.

Shirley: We loved those two people. They were remarkable! Later on, they came to visit us in our home here, and asked us to call them "Aunt Jessie and Uncle Joseph." We did. After that one of the apostles who wrote the Mormon doctrinal book, *A Marvelous Work and a Wonder,* visited us.

Pat: Throughout all of this, we could see that Cherry and the Mormon boy were becoming more deeply involved emotionally. He really had high hopes, and Cherry did too. So we began to talk to both of them—to Cherry about her commitment to Jesus Christ and her responsibility to hear His voice and obey Him—and to the boy about their need as a young couple to build their relationship on Jesus and His Word alone.

"I know there will never be anyone in my life but Cherry, and I hope to marry her," he said.

"But Cherry's not a member of the Mormon church," we objected." And that prevents you from marrying her, doesn't it?"

"All she has to do is read the book of Mormon and then pray and fast for three days and ask God to give her the witness that Mormonism is the truth, and that Joseph Smith is God's prophet," he said.

Shirley: Well, I was uneasy about the whole thing. We had just come out of a legalistic, rules-oriented church, and now we were being drawn toward *another* one. And this one got some of its doctrine from books other than the Bible! Pat and I prayed together, and I fasted and prayed a great deal alone.

Pat: Yes, we had great misgivings about it, sort of a sick feeling in our stomachs. It seemed so clear that what Cherry, or any of us, needed was just a simple *relationship* with Jesus, not a complicated *religion.* It seemed to us that if they were ever to be married, we needed to trust God to work with both of them, to show them His will and to help them do it. It was too crucial a matter for us to simply order her to break off with the boy.

Because Cherry loved this boy, she not only read the *Book of Mormon,* but *The Doctrines and Covenants, The Pearl of Great Price,* and other Mormon books. She read a lot more than most Mormons do—probably at least as much as her boyfriend had read. She came to know more about the Mormon faith than most Mormons I've met! But at the same time, she had her Bible open constantly—comparing what's taught there with what the *Book of Mormon* said. (I personally feel that the *Book of Mormon* has a ring of authority about it because a great portion of it is taken directly from the Bible. The rest is new and strange-sounding material Joseph Smith said God revealed to him. So if a person doesn't know his Bible well, he could easily say, "Man, this Mormon book *must* be from God. There's such a majesty and authority about it. No mere man, or group of men, could have made this up!" And as far as the Biblical parts are concerned, I'd agree with him!)

Shirley: But Cherry did everything her boyfriend asked of her. She even went to a Mormon Sunday School while she was reading the *Book of Mormon.* When she finished her study, she went on the three-day fast prescribed by the Mormon church. I don't mind saying I was deeply worried during this time. We prayed, and prayed again.

Pat: But when she finished the fast, Cherry had to tell her boyfriend, "I just don't get this witness that you want me to have. You and I agree on everything that the Bible teaches, but we disagree when we get away from the Bible."

"Look," he said. "This just can't be. There's something wrong. You're just not hearing what God wants you to hear. You're not open enough. Will you fast again?"

Shirley: So Cherry fasted another three days! This was a total of six days to get "this witness from God." Then a most remarkable thing happened.

Pat: Yes, it was astonishing. It had to be God! My secretary brought to us a cassette that had come in the mail from a man named Walter Martin. I didn't even know who he was at the time, but the label read, "Mormonism." Cherry found it in the kitchen. Not knowing whether it was pro or con, she decided to listen since this was the last day of her fast.

Shirley: I couldn't help overhearing what Martin was saying. It sounded so interesting I went in to listen with Cherry. What he said confirmed everything that she had been discovering— that so much of the Joseph Smith doctrine was contrary to the Bible. Yet this man Martin spoke with such obvious compassion and love for the Mormon people. He wasn't harsh and critical as so many are.

Finally, at the close of the tape he explained the reason for his study of the Mormon faith.

"You see, the blood of Brigham Young flows through my veins," he said. *"I am the great-grandson of Brigham Young."*

Pat: To Cherry that was God's answer to the six-day fast and all the searching of the past months. God had spoken to her clearly, unmistakably.

Shirley: The boy had wanted her to be baptized, and she had said, "Look, I *have* been baptized, into Jesus."

"But you need to be baptized by a priest. *I'm* a priest. Let me baptize you with the right authority."

A couple of nights later, when he came back expecting her to say that she had gotten her "witness," she had to break the news. She loved him so much, and it was obvious he loved her. Their anguish that night was dreadful.

Pat: Shirley and I were upstairs, but they were sobbing loudly enough that we could hear them. After an hour or so I even came down and walked noisily through the living room, hoping to distract them. When that failed, I went to the kitchen and banged around a bit, hoping the noise would temper their grief.

Shirley: Giving him up was so difficult, because he was such a good, sensitive person and treated her lovingly. Still, she knew it was hopeless, and that facing it now would be best for both of them. Later, through soul-wrenching sobs, Cherry asked, "Mama, do you think it's possible that there could ever be anybody better for me, or even as good?"

I was weeping too, but I assured her that one of two things would certainly happen: "Either the Lord will work through this heartache to help you both see that all either of you need is Jesus, His Word, and each other—or He's already preparing some young man for you *right this minute,* one who puts his trust in Jesus and not Joseph, and one you'll love even more. I know it!"

Pat: And you were right, Honey, more than you *could* know then.

Shirley: Well, that's what faith is, but it surely wasn't easy, for Cherry, or us, or the boy. I could still cry, thinking about it all.

Pat: Yes, it took several years for each to start dating again. But he finally found a beautiful girl, and I assume they're happily married. And Cherry? Well, we'll pick up her part of the story later.

Shirley: Afterward we learned that Walter Martin is a widely respected Bible teacher. He had heard that Cherry was going with a Mormon boy, so he sent this tape to Pat hoping that Cherry or someone would listen to it.

Pat: Eventually, we met at a conference at Melodyland Christian Center. Of course, I told him the story.

Shirley: We learned a valuable lesson from all this. We loved the people so much that we thought the church must be okay, too. For one thing, Mormonism was all new to us. And although we suspected there was something not quite right, with all the secret rituals and "latter-day prophets," still we thought that we could share our love for Jesus with this boy and his family.

Now we see a danger in this. If you allow yourself, or your children, to become involved in *any kind of religious doctrine that is not based solely on the Bible,* you're looking for trouble. Since then we have tried to spare our girls that kind of involvement. We've really tried to make them understand that dating boys who are not openly and totally committed to Jesus alone is a waste of time, and even potentially dangerous.

Pat: One of the problems was that this boy just didn't seem to be as open to Cherry's point of view as she was to his.

Cherry kept asking him: "If I've read all the books on Mormonism, why won't you just read the book of John?"

It was a fair request, but he refused. I woke up one night during this testing period (and I don't wake up at night). For nearly an hour Scripture verses kept running through my mind . . . "I am the way, the truth and the life . . . I am the vine and you are the branches . . . If you have seen Me, you have seen the Father . . . *The words that I speak,* they are spirit and they are life . . . he that has My commandments and keeps them, he it is that loves Me . . . if anyone loves Me he will keep My commandments."

I didn't know what to make of it right then, but there was this constant emphasis on Jesus and the Word of God. Finally, I went back to sleep again.

Next morning when I woke up, the experience came back to me clearly. And I saw it! We don't need a "further witness" from such people as Joseph Smith or Mary Baker Eddy or Ellen G. White or Sun Myung Moon. Maybe we could even get along without Peter, Paul and James if we had to, although I'm glad we have their writings.

But what the Lord showed me so clearly was the same message that He thundered audibly at the Mount of Transfiguration, "This is My beloved Son, with whom I am well pleased; hear Him" (Matthew 17:5)!

Peter and James and John were scurrying around, like we'd probably do, trying to do some "religious" things, build some monuments, make sure that nobody ever forgot the incredible thing that had just happened, and God stopped them cold! All He wanted them to do was listen to Jesus and do what He said.

And that's all He wants of any of us.

Of course, Mormonism isn't the only legalistic religion today; there are so many! And if you're willing to accept some other book than the Bible as your authority, *how will you choose between them?*

I sympathize with the millions of people who have been drawn into straight-jacket, judgmental religions, and I think I understand the basic reason. Most of us are pretty ignorant of what the Bible says, and we may feel we don't understand a lot of it.

So we welcome authority figures who tell us, "I have the answer! You don't have to study for yourself; I'll tell you what God wants you to know!"

And the sad part is, they usually make a lot of sense. Their motives may be good, and they mix Bible truth in with their own ideas and millions are led away from the simple Gospel.

It was already happening in Paul's day. Listen to what the Bible says, "Let me ask you this one question: Did you receive the Holy Spirit by trying to keep the Jewish laws? Of course not, for the Holy Spirit came upon you only after you heard about Christ and trusted Him as Savior. Then have you gone completely crazy? For if trying to obey the Jewish laws never gave you spiritual life in the first place, why do you think that trying to obey them now will make you stronger Christians? You have suffered so much for the Gospel. Now are you going to just throw it all overboard? I can hardly believe it! I ask you again, *does God give you the power of the Holy Spirit and work miracles among you* as a result of your trying to obey the Jewish laws? No, of course not. It is when you believe in Christ and fully trust Him" (Galatians 3:1-5 TLB).

Though Paul was referring specifically to the legalistic Jewish religion, the principle should be applied to any revelation or set of doctrinal rules today. We must obey Jesus' commandments, and only His, not the commands of men. And thank God, Jesus is so much more merciful than men are, particularly when He sees that a person's heart is right.

Surely that's what Paul was getting at in II Corinthians 3:6, "We do not tell them that *they must obey every law of God or die;* but we tell them there is life for them from the Holy Spirit. The old way, trying to be saved by keeping the Ten Commandments, *ends in death;* in the new way, the Holy Spirit gives them life" (TLB).

Praise God, we experienced these truths in our wilderness wandering. Jesus became so personal to us, and the Holy Spirit's ministry so precious and real, even though it was unsettling not to be part of a regular church fellowship. Right, Honey?

Shirley: Well, we began to feel like real vagabonds for a while—asked out of our church, running from others, and being criticized and warned by still others! We could really identify with Jesus going out into the wilderness. And there were others before Him—like Moses and Abraham, Isaac and Jacob—who struck out on their own to follow the Lord.

Wasn't there a simple, New Testament-style church home for us somewhere? Couldn't we just be part of a fellowship, a group of believers who were open to the Holy Spirit moving in our day and demonstrating the power of Jesus as He did in the first century?

There was. And we found it!

But first, Pat wants to tell you about an astonishing new direction, an incredible development in our lives.

5

Can You Live in Two Worlds Without a Split Personality?

PAT

What does a professional entertainer do to support his family after he really commits his life to the Lord?

Quit show biz and become a traveling evangelist?

Enroll in seminary and prepare for the ministry?

Become a gospel singer?

I got advice—and still do—from well-meaning Christians to do one or all of those things.

Now I know that God sometimes takes people out of their former professions when they become Christians, especially if they happen to have been prostitutes or criminals or something similar. But it seemed to me He had spent twenty years building a platform for me, and I didn't want to just walk off of it arbitrarily. If He *could* use me where I was, I wanted to give Him the opportunity.

I remembered that, when I was barely twenty years old, I had found myself smack in the middle of television and records and personal appearances, and also going to college and trying to raise a family. Just after I turned twenty-two, I was offered my own network television show, the youngest person ever to have such an opportunity. The only hitch was that the sponsor was a cigaret company.

"No," I said, "I can't be a cigaret salesman."

The answer was the same when, a few months later, I was offered another network show for a beer sponsor. It was so clear to me then, and the decision seemed simple, though I wanted very much to do my own show. And it was also clear to my agents and manager that I would probably be teaching school back in Tennessee before long.

But that didn't happen! Amazingly, other doors opened, and I found myself *hosting* my own television show for Chevrolet. Clearly, only God could have done it. *Maybe He wants to do something like that again,* I thought. It was worth a try.

But there were four major differences this time. When it first happened I had little to lose. Now I had four teenage daughters, who would be seriously affected by my choices.

The first inkling we had of what might be ahead came the summer after I finished writing *A New Song.* I had arranged a concert tour in Japan and had planned to take the Osmond Brothers, a musical group, with me. At the last minute Shirley agreed that she and the girls would go along. We had done a little singing together at home, and I had taken the whole family with me on a couple of TV shows as a lark. So I thought we might be able to cook up a song or two as a family.

It turned into a real family extravaganza! The whole Osmond family—with George and Olive, Jimmy and Marie, as well as the five singing brothers—went along with us. And we had a ball!

This was just before the Osmonds made their big records, but they were already known as semiregulars on the Andy Williams TV show. So when we put the Boone family and the Osmond family together in our Japanese performances, the crowds flipped out. We set attendance records all over Japan!

But that wasn't the best part. For the first time in my professional life, I had the wonderful experience of praying with fellow performers before each show. The Osmonds were a praying family too. Before each evening's work, we joined hands backstage and asked the Lord to bless what we did.

I was getting a glimpse of how good it could be for our family to travel and sing together. Obviously, it hadn't hurt the Osmonds. "Wicked ole show biz" wasn't tearing them apart. If anything, their working, singing and traveling together was welding them into an extremely close unit.

So when we got back home, I gave serious thought to launching out in a new direction. No pop singer had ever done it, and I realized it was a gamble, but I decided to take the plunge. With my agents we put together a trial concert tour to the smaller cities of Idaho and Utah, winding up in Eugene, Oregon.

Thus the Boone Family Show was launched.

At least we can try it out, I thought. *If it doesn't work, not many people will see the flop.*

Well, it was a real see-saw experience. The opening night was good. A full house and warm reception. We thought we were on to something big. But then for the next few nights, the auditoriums were only half full, and the critical response was less than enthusiastic. I was about to drop the whole idea when we got to Eugene, Oregon, on our last night.

MacArthur Center at the University of Oregon was packed with almost seven thousand people! We couldn't figure out where they all came from! Our sponsors, the good folks at Willamette Christian Center, had obviously done a great job of promoting. Shirley and I sang our hearts out, and so did the girls, then 15, 14, 13 and 12. They were amateurs, of course, but very appealing.

Audiences seemed to feel something good when they saw a real family working and singing together, and expressing their love for Jesus in music. I was convinced that we had "stumbled" onto something promising. But all of it had to be tabled while the girls went back to school at the end of the summer, and I met my own busy schedule of engagements.

But the following summer we planned a full concert tour of the Orient—Japan, Bangkok, Singapore, Manila, Seoul and Taiwan. We weren't pulling out all the stops; we were putting them in!

"That's when we found out our kids were real troupers!" Shirley says.

It was a murderous tour. We did twenty-eight shows in thirty days, and the concert halls were packed everywhere, especially at the army and navy bases! Those sailors and soldiers loved our four teenage daughters and raised the roof every time they came on stage or finished a song. And often there were tears in their eyes when we finished our show with some Jesus music, singing together as a family who really "had their act together."

Since this was a new thing for us, I had laid out some ground rules in advance. We had formed a traveling company of musicians and singers called Love Volume 8, six guys and two girls. Most of them were Christians. Following the pattern of our Japan tour, we often had prayer before our shows and occasional worship times at our hotel. On Sundays we always tried to have a communion service. These turned out to be emotional times, because some of our musicians had never experienced such intimate worship and sharing. We all came back from the tour, tired but better people. And our family was closer than ever.

Now came a big test. My last contracted appearance in Las Vegas was coming up. Did I dare to make it a family outing?

Oh, the family had been with me when I had played Las Vegas the summer before. Not singing, just "along for the ride." We had rented Phyllis Diller's home and thoroughly enjoyed its kooky luxuries. But of course I didn't get home from work until two o'clock in the morning. Then because I had to sleep, the rest of the family had to tiptoe around until I got up around ten or eleven.

Shirley and I talked it over. "The girls are older now. Perhaps it would be all right to take them with us to the hotel and do the first show as a family," she said.

The girls loved the idea, so we agreed that whenever they felt like doing the show with me, they would do it. Otherwise I would have an alternate show ready.

The first night, they not only did the first show, but also the second show. It didn't close until 1:30 a.m.! From then on it was a breeze—fifty-six shows without stopping and no days off. Twenty-eight nights in a row, and they loved it! On top of that, we set an all-time record attendance for the hotel during that period.

People are just people! Surprise, surprise! We were discovering that, whether we were in Manila or Minneapolis, Las Vegas or Taiwan—people respond favorably to family entertainment.

And we had fun in Phyllis Diller's house! I described it then as decorated in "early asylum." For some reason the wall sockets were all shoulder high, so I explained "Phyllis had them installed at that height so she could stick her finger in the sockets without bending over. That's the way she does her hair." And so on.

That summer was a terrific family time, because we were all on the same schedule together. We got home at 2:00 a.m., grabbed a little snack out of the refrigerator, laughed and prayed together and went to bed. We all got up before noon, had breakfast and some devotional time. Cherry and I would jog, and then we'd all splash it up in Phyllis's pool. There was a coed gym not far away, and most of us (except Shirley) went over there about three times a week. An early dinner, usually at the hotel, and we did our two shows a night.

Often people came back to our dressing room after the shows and made statements like, "You had me in tears. I don't know what it was, but I really felt something while you were singing. I hope you'll keep it up."

Sometimes the discussions got deeper than that, and though

Phyllis Diller may not know it, we used her pool as a baptistry more than once!

I could tell that what was happening was good for us, and evidently for others too. I wondered if God was showing me a pattern for our lives, for at least the next several years. Still because of much criticism from well-meaning Christians (who had never seen our show, but were convinced that the entertainment business was sinful, especially if it took us to Las Vegas), Shirley was doubtful.

Then one day she got a call from a girl who worked for our next door neighbor in Beverly Hills. According to this young woman, her grandmother was a godly person. Her grandfather, on the other hand, was a feisty man with little interest in spiritual things. They "happened" to be in Las Vegas while we were performing there, so they came to see our act.

"For many years my grandmother prayed for my grandfather," the girl told Shirley. "But nothing happened. That night your family sang the song, 'I Wish We'd All Been Ready.' That was the turning point for my grandfather. Shortly after that he accepted Christ as his Savior." Then she added, "And now, he's gone to be with Jesus."

Next came our first big television appearance—with Flip Wilson!

Flip was great to work with, and we laughed ourselves silly with him for six days of rehearsals. We had a major portion of the show, and it all turned out well. A few days after the show aired on TV, I got a call from his producer, Bob Henry.

"Thought you'd be interested to know," he said, "that this particular 'Flip Wilson Show' got the highest rating we've ever had—a 60 percent share of the audience! And frankly—don't take this wrong—I don't know what to make of it. We've had Bing Crosby, Lucille Ball, Bill Cosby and all kinds of other big performers with us, and we really can't figure out why this show got such a rating."

And then he went on to tell me that when the show started, the ratings showed "only a 50 percent audience share; but by the time the show ended, it had gone up to the 60 percent!" Now this is incredible. Bob told me that it indicated lots of people must have phoned friends and told them, "You've got to see this show. Turn to the 'Flip Wilson Show' with the Boone family."

I didn't know what to make of it either, but I glanced upward and smiled.

The snowball kept rolling after this. We did the "Glen Campbell Show" and then a TV special with Bob Hope, Carol Channing, Raymond Burr, Charley Pride and the cream of the entertainment world. I'll never forget my four girls, with their limited experience, walking out on that stage in front of the TV cameras to sing a song with Bob Hope. I was more nervous than they were!

But don't get me wrong. It wasn't all gravy. One night after one of our shows, a handsome, young musician edged up to Cherry, not realizing (or caring, maybe) that her mother was part of the same group standing there.

"That was a great show," he said. "You sing good, and you look even better. Why don't we cut out? I can have you wherever you need to be tomorrow morning."

Cherry sputtered, "I'm staying with my parents and my sisters."

"Oh, sure, I know that. But you're grown; you can do what you want, can't you? Come on, we'll have some fun."

By this time Shirley got wind of what was happening. "Girls, it's time to head for the hotel," she said.

This and many other situations confronted the girls backstage and other places, while we traveled and sang. They were a constant concern for Shirley and me.

So we continued to struggle with the question: did we as a Christian family belong in the entertainment profession?

6

Tempest in the
Family Teapot

SHIRLEY & PAT

Pat: It's rough enough to try to raise a family these days at home; you should try it on the road!

Shirley: Yes, the topsy-turvy schedule of our lives these last few years has made things very complex. First of all, we wanted our girls to have a "normal" school life, so we decided to take them out of school to do some singing only on rare occasions—then during the summer, we'd be gone for three or four weeks at a stretch, sometimes longer.

Pat: And in addition to school problems, being away on singing tours can cause problems with a teenage girl's love life! Of course, as a protective father, I'd always liked the idea of my girls being "moving targets."

Shirley: From the very beginning, I've tried to see that our girls didn't become typical "entertainers' kids." I don't mean to criticize the way other entertainers raise their families, but it has seemed clear to us that entertainers' careers often come first, and children second or third. As a result, we've seen so many of those young people becoming self-reliant on the surface, almost selfish, and seemingly indifferent to the love, to the desires, or discipline of their parents.

Pat: Discipline—*what* discipline? From what I've seen, most entertainers let their kids do anything they want to!

Shirley: Yes, I guess we have been strict with our kids, but I think that's because of our Christian upbringing, and the way *our* parents made us toe the mark. We decided, early in the game, that we were not going to let Hollywood standards influence the raising of our family. We'd do it *our* way, and God's way, as best we could understand it. But that's a lot easier said than done.

Pat: The pressures out here in this environment are tremendous, especially on teenage kids—not just drugs and sex. From the earliest school days, we've had to fight the influence of other kids on ours that made them rebel against our way of doing things and demand the right to do "what the other kids do."

Shirley: Does that sound familiar to other parents anywhere? Maybe our problems as entertainer-parents are not so different from other people's. For instance, I remember that we had a serious problem with Cherry over makeup long before any of us thought about joining you on stage!

Pat: Boy, did we! Cherry was our first-born, the oldest, and maybe we were more strict with her than the others. I guess that often happens with the oldest. That makeup problem was a lulu. For some reason, which I've never understood, Cherry wanted to load that black gook on her eyelashes, some red paste on her cheeks, and then try to hide her lips under a quarter pound of red margarine—at least, that's the way it looked to me. She was so naturally pretty that I couldn't stand seeing all of that phony camouflage. Over and over, this was the script:

"Cherry, you've got on too much mascara; I thought I told you about that."

"Daddy, I've got on just a little bit."

"I'm telling you, it's too much. Go upstairs and take most of it off."

Before she got upstairs the mascara would be running down her cheeks in muddy, black tears, and we'd be late to wherever we were going. It was very, very exasperating.

Shirley: I sympathized with Cherry and really didn't think the makeup problem was so crucial. But in short order, it was obvious that makeup was only part of the problem. There seemed to be real difficulties between Cherry and Pat, rebellion on her part, an insistence on having her way, and perhaps (I say "perhaps") Pat was a little too unyielding. Looking back, I believe Cherry was just in the normal teenage pattern of self-assertion, and maybe a little rebellion. Makeup was only a symptom.

Pat: Yes, Honey, I'd like to go back and relive those days. Maybe I should have let Cherry do her "clown number," and just have taken some Polaroid pictures to show her how she was hiding her natural beauty. The awful thing is, I think she actually *liked* the way she looked then!

I'm sure that one of the big reasons I got so uptight was that this episode came *after* we'd all been filled with the Holy Spirit. I didn't expect my Spirit-filled kids to get their backs up at Daddy that way. I see now that I was leaving out the human factor too much.

Shirley: I know that Cherry wanted to please you. She'd always been impressed with the record you made at Columbia University, magna cum laude and all. She drove herself to be number one in *her* classes, from the first grade on.

You know, Pat, I was just looking over the girls' report cards the other day, some of them from way back. I ran across this teacher's comments on one of Cherry's cards: "You are overworking yourself. You got an *A* long before you quit."

So there was a real conflict going on in Cherry—a sincere desire to please Pat and me, to please the Lord, but also to be herself and to be accepted by her friends, especially the boys. It was a real tug of war. It's not easy for any teenage girl these days.

Actually, when we did join Pat in his stage work, the girls got plenty of chances to wear makeup, and were usually happy when they didn't have to! I think that was a bonus.

Pat: My run-ins with Cherry seem minor league compared to the head-on collisions I had with Debby! She's our third daughter, the only blonde in the group. Psychologists tell me that the third child is often the most individualistic, not wanting to be a carbon copy of either the first or the second. They want to be themselves! Debby's always been like that.

Shirley: Of all the girls, I think Debby hated school the most. She often had tense relations with her teachers. You've always been able to read what Debby felt right on her face. If she resented an assignment or some discipline in class, she could not hide it from the teacher.

We were always getting notes from school that "Debby should make more of an effort to cooperate with the class." Or "Debby's attitude needs improving."

Pat: This was really throwing me for a loop, because Cherry and Lindy had always gotten along so well at school, and the teachers all loved them. Year by year, we had the same sad song with Debby. She'd come home from school, upset and in tears, saying something like, "I just can't stand that woman! She doesn't like anything I do. She doesn't like me."

Quite often, I'd have a talk with her.

"Debby, why don't you talk to her after class and tell her that you're sorry about the conflicts, that you really do want to do the work and make good grades. Ask her what you need to do to please her."

Once in a while, she'd tell me that she had done that, but it didn't seem to help. I think now that Debby felt unsure of herself in school, may have felt unable to match Cherry and Lindy in their scholastic achievements. She decided that she hated the whole school and homework experience. Naturally, this attitude was obvious to her teachers, and, being human, they reacted in negative ways. It seemed to be a vicious circle.

Shirley: I guess all kids go through a rebel stage, when they're asserting their own personalities and testing their wings. But Debby was a hard nut to crack. She had a tough time taking instructions from her dad.

When Pat would tell her to do something, or tell her she couldn't do something, she would give him this sullen look, with her eyes at half-mast. Or maybe, she wouldn't look at him at all.

Pat: And that made me madder than anything. As long as we could talk about it, I could take some sour looks. But when she appeared to be thinking about something else, shutting me out, I really saw red.

Several times Debby told her sisters, "As soon as I turn eighteen I'm going to get myself a motorcycle and move up to my own apartment in San Francisco."

When I heard about that, it worried me a lot.

Shirley: Trouble was, her actions spoke louder than her words. She didn't need to say anything; her sullen expression would tell exactly how she felt.

Pat: Yes, sometimes when she turned that grim gargoyle look on me, I'd grab her by the back of the neck and push her over in front of the mirror.

"Look at yourself," I'd say. "Look at that. Isn't that a beautiful picture?"

The effect was usually the opposite of what I wanted; she'd be livid with rage and convulsed in tears.

Eventually, the Lord got through to me by His Word, "Fathers, provoke not your children to wrath."

I knew I was doing something wrong, but in my exasperation, I couldn't figure out what it was. I know that a father is to use his authority, and that kids are to obey—but what do you do when that formula doesn't work?

Shirley: I spent long hours talking with Debby, trying to heal the breach between her and her father. She would sit and look at me, but I could never tell whether I was getting through. She felt her father was too strict with her, that he expected more of her than he did of the others.

Pat: I realized when I heard this that attitude was the real problem. Maybe mine, as well as hers.

The amazing thing was that Debby would come home from school and ask Shirley and me to pray for one or another of her friends!

"Two of my best friends are starting to smoke marijuana. I know they're going to get loused up. Can we pray together for them?" she'd ask.

Here she'd be so rebellious in the evening, and then so obviously concerned about spiritual things the very next day! I saw that her attitude toward her friends was different from her attitude toward me.

So we prayed together for her friends. And we saw miracles happen! A few days after we prayed for one who was starting to get messed up with drugs, that friend came up to Debby at school. She was obviously in great distress.

"I need your help, Deb. Will you pray for me?"

She and Debby wound up in tears and prayed together. Later, that girl told Debby she had decided marijuana was not for her, and she gave it up. It was a time of rejoicing around our house, and it was a wonderful experience for Debby.

Shirley: Remember the time Debby asked us to pray for a girlfriend who had been given permission by her parents to go to Las Vegas with a boyfriend for a weekend with him—alone? As I remember the young pair went ahead with their plans. Though that was disappointing to Deb and to us, it deepened her concern for her friend. More than once she's fasted and prayed for her, and has since seen that girl commit her life to Jesus!

Pat: And yet, there was this rebellion right in the middle of these happy spiritual experiences. Where in the world was it coming from?

One day, walking past her room, I froze. She and Lindy were sharing a room, and I suddenly realized that the room itself was completely out of place in our house! Debby had gradually pasted up pictures and psychedelic posters all over the room, until it almost looked like a "head shop," a store catering to rock and pot-trippers. She had pictures of Jimmy Hendrix and Janis Joplin, both of whom died of drug overdoses, and lots of pictures of kids and rock musicians apparently "breaking out" of organized society and traditional inhibitions. The room was colorful certainly, but it had also a bizarre quality that made me uneasy.

Shirley: Lindy, since it was also her room, had put up a few Scripture quotations and a picture of Jesus, and little things like that. But Debby had virtually taken the room over. I'm sure she just wanted to express her own individuality, but Pat and I both felt she was starting to head in the wrong direction.

Pat: So at first I tried to kid Debby about it. To keep it light. I'd walk into the room and ask seriously, "Is Mick Jagger home?" Or "Excuse me, I'm freaking out. Is this a good place to crash?"

Or I'd walk over to the pictures and stand there admiringly, "Ah, Jimmy and Janis, my idols! Why did you leave us so soon? The young people of America need you!"

This just didn't seem to get it. In fact, it seemed to widen the gap.

Shirley: For a while, it was like living with two people—the sweet, young blonde who would want to pray for her friends, and the tight-lipped rebel who spent hours alone in her room with the door closed, listening to rock music by herself.

Pat: Well, I was praying a lot about it, and one day while she was at school, I went into her room and pinned up a picture of Jesus in the middle of a psychedelic collage! It was a tiny picture, almost unnoticeable. I prayed as I did it.

Then I walked around the room and found a couple of other inconspicuous places to put up a Scripture verse, a line or two from a poem, and a little symbolic fish. I felt I was doing it tastefully, not spoiling the collage, and that maybe these few reminders would temper the impact of the rest of the material on the walls. I prayed that Jesus would speak to her through those additions.

And then I walked around the room, rebuking Satan in Jesus' name and cutting off any spiritual influence he might have on Debby's rebellion. Shirley and a friend joined me in this prayer.

Shirley: The results were not exactly as we expected. When Debby got home from school, she was furious. She tore down all the pictures, both hers and Pat's. Then she locked herself in her bathroom, crying. She felt that Pat had ruined everything and that her privacy had been violated terribly.

Pat: I just let her stay in there for a while, and I sat out in her room, wondering if I had done the right thing. Then I noticed a curious thing. The room felt clean! Ragged, but clean. And it was Debby who had torn all the stuff down!

I just smiled, quietly thanked the Lord, and left. Several days of strained silence went by.

Shirley: But there was a noticeable difference in Debby after that. She never put all those psychedelic things back up, and gradually we saw more and more of the little blonde who was concerned about her friends, and the Lord, and her appearance.

Today Debby says that taking those posters and all that psychedelic art down from her walls did affect her spiritually. She realizes now that the constant reminders of rebellion all around her were shaping her attitudes.

Pat: That principle goes back to God's admonition to the people of Israel when they were getting ready to go into Canaan, "Tear down all their temples of worship and destroy their idols!"

As long as the Israelites obeyed, they conquered their enemies. But when they left pagan places of worship and idols intact, they got into trouble!

First, they probably just passed by and smiled at these idols. Later, they stopped to look at them more closely, and wondered what good they were. Finally, they found themselves worshipping them! It was not that they failed to worship God but that they included pagan paraphernalia and practices in their worship of Jehovah! God knew that these things would eventually divert His people.

And the same thing can happen to us. I realize we can get hung up on externals, and I certainly don't have a case against hard rock music, or all posters, or movies or things like that. But a steady diet of worldly things can wear us down spiritually, without our even realizing it.

I'll tell you how far we've taken it at our house. We invited some of the elders from Church on the Way to come to our home. We went through the whole house, looking for anything pagan or anti-Christ in nature. We've traveled a lot and brought back souvenirs from around the world. We were amazed at how many idol-statues, paintings and trinkets we had lying around. I had gathered books from here and there on occult religions and cults because I'd bump into those things so often. But I decided I didn't need anything but the Word of God to withstand those things. We burned the books. (One of these days I may toss out our TV set!)

Shirley: What do you do about influences at school, though? We've really had our hands full there. These days, it's not just their friends that we're worried about, but some of the assignments from their teachers!

Pat: That's really driven me up the wall. Not just the subject matter, but the tremendously heavy work load, too. I don't know if this is true everywhere, but in the school where our girls spent most of their high school years, there was such emphasis given to college preparation that they were nearly killing the girls off before they got there!

I spoke up at several PTA meetings.

"I believe these girls are being given too much homework. When they get home from school, they immediately go to their rooms and work all afternoon and evening. We have to force them to go to bed a lot of times because they're worried about unfinished homework. Then they often get up early and work until time for school again. *I* don't work that hard!"

There was some discussion between the principal and some of the other parents. Then I made my final statement.

"I'm all for scholarship and expecting the best of our kids, but I believe they need some time for rest, play, and plain old day-dreaming, too. If we can't make some real reductions in their homework assignments, I'm afraid I'll have to put our girls in another school, much as I dislike the idea."

Afterwards many other parents voiced similar concerns to me. One father stood back until the evening was almost finished, and then approached me.

"That was all very brave of you," he said, "and I sympathize. My daughter has to work too hard, too. But a lot of it was hot air. You and I know you're not about to tell your daughter where she's going to school! She'll make that decision for herself."

I looked at him in amazement. "Maybe at *your house* your daughter makes those decisions, but where my daughter's future good is concerned, I'm her father, and *I* make the final decisions."

And eventually, I did take our younger two daughters out of that school.

Shirley: But really, Pat, the work load was not the only reason. We were more concerned because they were being assigned books and plays to read that were just this side of pornographic. And some of the teachers were arranging for after-hours showings of x-rated films for some of the students, because of "cultural content."

Pat went to school a couple of afternoons to see the films and came home furious about the macabre, bizarre and dehumanizing quality of some of them. The girls had been assigned to see some films written and produced by mental patients!

Pat: I was ready to take my girls out of school entirely and move to the wilds of Canada or somewhere. Then came the final straw. Debby was assigned the book *Soul On Ice* by Eldridge Cleaver. It was a best seller by the black militant leader, and I had read it myself. I jumped into my car and drove to the school, taking Debby with me.

"My daughter is not going to read that book," I told the teacher. "If she were in college, it would be one thing. But she's fifteen years old, and I don't intend for her to read the pornographic fantasies of a convicted rapist. What is your reason for assigning it to fifteen- and sixteen- year-old girls in the first place?"

"Don't you know that these kids have already bought this on the stands and are reading it?" he asked. "Don't you think it's better to discuss it in a classroom under a teacher's supervision?"

"No, siree, I don't!" I was trying to stay cool. "There are a lot of other things these kids will get into after school hours—things like drugs and sex—and I hope you're not intending to bring those activities into the classroom and grade the kids on them! It's one thing for kids to probe and investigate on their own, without our permission or approval; it's quite another to make them classroom assignments and grade them!"

Incredibly, some years later Eldridge Cleaver voluntarily returned from exile and told a shocked America about his total transformation by Jesus. Recently, he and Kathleen joined us for dinner in our home, and he agreed with me that his book should never have been read by teenage girls under any circumstances. I was grateful for his confirmation.

The teacher and I argued on the subject for at least an hour. He was just as sure of his point of view as I was of mine. Finally, he turned to Debby.

"What do you think, Debby?" he asked. Can you handle this book?" I'm sure he thought Debby would say she could.

To my amazement, Debby, the rugged individualist, the girl who wanted to express herself and do her own thing, took a minute or so to deliberate and finally spoke.

"I'd really rather not have to make a decision about this right now. I'm having to make up my mind about a lot of other heavy things, like immigration laws and integration, as well as math and science. I think I've got all I can handle right now. I'd rather leave this until later."

Her answer stopped the teacher cold. He assigned her

another book to fulfill her assignment. Still, I felt the handwriting was on the wall. I took her and Laury out of that school and put them into a Catholic school. Things would be different there, I thought.

Shirley: But we were in for more surprises. Even in the Catholic schools, the social and public pressure has become too strong for the teachers to handle. As we checked with the girls about their homework assignments (as we always have), we discovered that they were having to read similar junk, because it's considered "modern literature."

One day Laury brought home a book on marriage relationships. She mentioned that a couple of chapters were "sort of embarrassing," so I asked her to let me see it. I quickly handed it to Pat.

Pat: I was flabbergasted. Obviously, the intent of the book was to present a complete and balanced picture of marriage attitudes and relationships. But one whole chapter was given over to a detailed account of a wife's sexual feelings toward her husband, her preparations throughout the day so that they could have satisfying intercourse in the evening. The second chapter was a detailed account, stage by stage, of his and her arousals, what their feelings were and concluded with a description of the mutual climax and their feelings afterwards.

This time I went to see the principal and the nun who was teaching the class. Both of them were red-faced and somewhat apologetic.

"Let's face it, Mr. Boone," they said, "many of our girls are already involved in sexual activity. We know that, and we feel that if we can give them a picture of what we believe sex in marriage really should be, they'll at least have a better perspective."

"I understand your thinking," I said, "but let me be very frank with you. By the time I finished reading this second chapter, I needed some kind of an outlet for the feelings that had been kindled in *me.* I can just imagine how these teenage girls will react. In the book the man and wife have both been satisfied, but the girls who read about it won't be. Don't you think they also are going to look around for some way to be gratified?

"Sisters, I'm afraid this approach will accomplish the very thing you're trying to prevent. A large part of the joy of marriage is discovery and exploration, and a certain mystique. Surely, you can present a balanced picture of marriage and love relationships without going into all these details, before the girls are anywhere near ready to experience those things—at least scripturally and morally."

Shirley: I'm sure a lot of these problems sound familiar to you, if you're trying to raise a family, no matter where you live. Through the trials, we've discovered an important fact: *God invented the family, and He's concerned about the way it works.* That's one of the reasons the Holy Spirit is so necessary today in any family. Romans 5:5 says that "God's kind of love is shed abroad in our hearts by the Holy Spirit who is given to us." I don't see how a family can make it today without the daily help of the Holy Spirit, working in and through each member of the family.

God and the parents are not the only ones interested in the family—so is the devil. He's interested in destroying the whole arrangement, and every member of the family, if he can.

We knew this from our study of the Bible and the minor skirmishes we had with him right at home. But when we started traveling and singing as a family, Satan confronted us head-on in the middle of the road!

7
Targets of the Devil

PAT

"Daddy, it looks like Jill and I are the only two virgins left."
Laury was only fifteen, and made the statement with such
a matter-of-fact air that I had trouble focusing on it at first. It
was late spring and the weather was beautiful, even after 6:30 in
the evening. Our family had just finished dinner, and Laury
had asked if I'd like to shoot a little basketball with her. I refused to admit that I had reached the age where I didn't like
the idea of playing basketball immediately after dinner, so I
went out back with her.

We had recently finished a short concert tour with the
family, and the girls were back in school. Laury was alternately on the basketball and volleyball teams, and was having to
work extra hard to keep up with the others. She's a terrific
all-round athlete, so we hustled, dribbled, shot and rebounded
for quite a while.

"How do you know that?" I asked, trying to be as casual
about it as she was.

"Oh, we all talk about it in our group of friends," she
answered. "Most of the girls sort of brag about their ex-

periences, and once in a while one of them gets pretty torn up because her boyfriend dumps her. And, of course, the girls talk about each other a good bit, so after a while you can run down the list and keep score!"

I decided to probe a little. "But isn't a lot of that just talk? I remember when I was in school the boys, at least, used to brag about their experiences with girls, and I was always a bit envious—until I realized that they were making up most of it."

"Well," she said, "I guess that's possible. But really, Daddy, the girls aren't bragging because it's so common these days. It's really expected, and most of the parents have already arranged for their girls to have the pill. One or two of my friends have actually come home from school in the afternoon unexpectedly, and discovered their mothers with other men, once actually in bed! Several of my friends' parents are divorced, and their moms date first one guy and then another. No, it's not just talk. The other girls think Jill and I are slow, or something."

A fact kept thumping in my brain, louder and louder: *this girl is just fifteen years old!* This is our baby, a girl in a Christian home, in a "Christian" school, and standing out like a sore thumb because she is still virgin! I wanted to cry; was the world really this sick already?

I asked her one more question. "How does it make you feel, Laury?"

She took a couple more shots and answered, "I just feel sorry for my friends, Daddy. They think they're having fun, and I guess they are—for now. But I know there's a price to pay for that, and that most of them are in for some real heartaches and disappointments. I don't know if their consciences will ever hurt them, but I know mine would.

"Also, I feel a little special. I know I'm not, except that there don't seem to be many girls around my age who are still virgins, especially because they *want* to be. And I feel like that makes me a little different, maybe a little special."

Now I did cry! More inwardly than visibly, but I've wept and praised the Lord a lot since then. I've thanked Him for His special protection and guidance in keeping our girls focused on Him and His will for their lives, without making them "sticks-in-the-mud" or fanatics or weirdos. My daughters aren't robots; they make their own decisions because they have to. When they make different choices than other girls their age, it's because they have a different set of priorities, not because of ignorance or naivete.

But the pressures! I'm sure it's true where you live, too, because the world is selling out in a wholesale way. But here in Hollywood where fifteen-year-old kids have their own cars, are allowed to spend weekends together, where parents sometimes go away for months at a time, and leave their kids to shift for themselves, where drugs and sex are as openly available as cafeteria lunches—it's a spiritual swamp for teenagers.

Debby told me about one of her friends at school.

"She and her boyfriend decided to see how many sins they could commit in an hour. They went to her house after school and smoked pot, took some pills, had sex, drank some booze, used every swear word they could think of—and still had fifteen minutes left over."

The story was so absurd that I almost laughed. But then I realized that this was true, and Debby wasn't laughing. Her friend had laughed when she told Debby the story, and the girls standing around had too, but the very fact that everybody else was laughing hilariously made Debby realize how serious it was. She didn't preach a sermon, or put her friend down, but she couldn't laugh.

More than one of our daughters' close friends have shared their home bedrooms with boys for extended periods of time, with their parents' permission! When one of Cherry's best friends was still in her teens, her parents brought home a size-able cache of marijuana, spread it out on the kitchen table and said to her and her brother, "We're all gonna' get high together. Why should you kids be having all the fun?"

Now, I'm nobody's judge. I don't know what was going through the minds of these other parents. But I do know Paul says that the mystery of lawlessness is already at work, but he himself (the anti-Christ prophet, the satanic messiah) will not come until the One who is holding him back (the Holy Spirit) steps out of the way. Then this wicked one will appear, whom the Lord Jesus will burn up with the breath of His mouth and destroy by His presence when He returns.

This man of sin will come as Satan's tool and will trick everyone with strange demonstrations, and will do great miracles. He will completely fool those who are on their way to hell because they have said no to the truth; they have refused to believe it, love it and let it save them. So God will allow them to believe lies and will judge them for it (II Thessalonians 2:7-12).

Our kids are being bombarded everyday through TV, magazines, newspapers and friends—and sometimes even ministers—with lies straight out of hell. But these ideas sound so good and reasonable and humane that our kids believe them. Yes, I refer even to ministers, because Paul says, "But the Spirit explicitly says that in later times some will fall away from the faith, paying attention to deceitful spirits and doctrines of demons, by means of the hypocrisy of liars seared in their own conscience as with a branding iron" (I Timothy 4:1,2).

More and more, we're reading quotes from ministers and religious people in various walks of life who are saying, "Young people should live together before they're married; how else will they know if they're compatible? As long as their intentions are to get married, we should encourage them. They'll have better marriages because of it."

Just yesterday, I was on television in a heated discussion with the founder of the world's largest homosexual church. He's an ordained minister, and he claims that God created many people homosexual. Therefore, all the Scriptures which prohibit homosexuality apply only to heterosexuals, not to "gay" men and women to whom God has given a "special gift."

I tried to help him see that God did give homosexuals something, according to Romans 1. He gave them over to impurity (vs. 24), degrading passions (vs. 26), depraved minds (vs.

28), and finally, a death penalty (vs. 32). But since this minister has already committed himself to what God calls in Leviticus 18 an abomination, and is himself a leader in this movement, he couldn't hear or receive what I was saying, even though it's right out of the Bible.

And I had the sinking feeling that most of the people in the studio (and possibly a lot of the viewers) felt he was entitled to his opinions, and that I was voicing an outworn religious taboo. Why shouldn't they think that, when mainline churches are now ordaining homosexual women as priests?

How are Christian parents, Bible-believing mothers and dads, supposed to teach their kids right and wrong?

Well, Shirley and I were glad that the Lord had nudged us out onto the road, and that we were spending a good bit of time rehearsing and singing and traveling together as a family, with just enough time at home for the girls to keep up with their school. And they·had to work so hard then that they didn't have time for mischief!

Then we discovered that we had picked up a hitch-hiker. The devil himself had come to ride with us.

First, he wormed his way into our musical group and split them up. I had put together a small band of Christian musicians, but we hadn't been traveling long when they began to squabble among themselves. I had to start all over. It was a tremendous disappointment to me, and it wasn't until later that I realized that Satan, as a stow-away, had sowed division and strife in our group.

Since I was aware of how difficult it is for Christians to get along with each other sometimes, I decided to put together a group of good professional musicians, and hoped they'd become Christians on down the road someplace. That was a mistake too! It went smoothly for a while, but then the individual habits of otherwise fine young men began to make for a rocky ride.

I discovered that my conductor and our drummer were deeply involved in Transcendental Meditation. I took what opportunity I had to discuss it with them, but I figured it was their business, and eventually they would phase out of that if they heard the Gospel message enough times. But one day on our chartered bus, I did a fast double take. Was that Laury sitting cross-legged on the back seat, her eyes closed, and her hands resting on her knees, palms upward? Was that a "lotus position"?

I headed for the back of the bus, jerked her over to the side of the seat, and asked in a harsh whisper, "What do you think you're doing?"

She was startled, somewhat flustered, but innocently answered, "I was just meditating. Is there anything wrong with that?"

We had a long talk, bouncing along in the back of the bus, about the differences between meditating "on the law of the Lord," communing with Jesus, and praying—and the Hindu practice of self-realization and attainment by meditating on nothing. Christian meditation focuses attention on God, on His will for us, and on His presence. The other is part of a pagan religion, which teaches that man may arrive at God-status himself by chanting, meditating and "growing holy."

Laury understood, and admitted that she had picked up this seemingly innocent practice from our musicians. While she was talking, I saw a couple of astrology magazines on the seat beside her. The musicians had brought those on board, too, and liked to work on their charts and talk about people's "signs." I knew right then we would be forming a new musical group! And we did, at the end of that trip.

But that very night Laury fainted on stage! Toward the end of our family performance, she just keeled over backwards and hit the floor with a thud. One of our singers, Ernie Retino, scooped her up and carried her off-stage to a dressing room. We were in Ogden, Utah, singing to a packed house, and the show had been going well until then. Somehow we closed ranks, finished our closing song, took hurried bows and ran backstage. The enthusiastic crowd let us go, sensing that we had sung as much as we were going to, under the circumstances.

Backstage, we all gathered around Laury and prayed for her fervently. Almost immediately, she stirred, looked around, smiled at us and got up! She had a slight headache (from the big lump on the back of her head), but slept well and felt great from then on. But before she went to bed that night, we prayed about the whole situation, talked about her fiddling with Transcendental Meditation and astrology, and how she might have opened herself to some spiritual harassment. Laury has always been sensitive to spiritual things, both good and bad. She herself asked the Lord to forgive her for any ignorant transgression and to seal off any place she might have given, unintentionally, to the devil.

You may think this all sounds a little far-fetched. Let me assure you it's not. Check Matthew 16:15-23 and you'll see Jesus commending Peter for being sensitive to the Spirit of God and then rebuking Satan for his influence on Peter.

In just a matter of minutes, Peter, a beloved disciple of Jesus, was receptive to God's revelation *and* Satan's spiritual influence. Parents, don't fool yourselves; Satan has not stopped this kind of activity. And he doesn't wait until our kids grow up before he starts trying to destroy them.

Just yesterday in my TV encounter with the homosexuals, one of them told me he had been a homosexual since birth.

"By the time I was three years old, I was having romantic fantasies about men, and even imagining erotic experiences with them. Doesn't that prove I was born a homosexual?"

"It proves two things," I said. "You had a normal fertile imagination, and it naturally centered on the people who were strong influences on you at that early age, in your case, men. It also proves that Satan took a special interest in you while you were still an infant, and whispered or suggested things to your spirit that were reflected in your thoughts and dreams."

If Satan did it to Peter, why would he not do it to any of us?

And if his goal is the destruction of humanity, why shouldn't he pick on babies and children? Why should yours be exempt—or mine?

Satan is especially effective working through our "reasoning" and our good human motives. Peter's motive was to prevent Jesus from going to Jerusalem, where the Lord had said He would be sacrificed. Peter thought he was being considerate and protective, but Jesus saw him as an obstacle to God's will.

Another of our musicians convinced Debby that she should be a vegetarian. I know he meant well, and he didn't see any spiritual implications at all. He realized that we often eat ignorantly and fail to have nutritional balance, and he was really gung ho on vegetables.

I didn't think much about it at first when Debby decided she would no longer eat meat. Ironically, she had been our biggest meat-eater, able to put away a couple pounds of prime rib at one sitting! Now she really got serious about vegetables and nuts and fruits, and I figured that was okay.

Shirley checked out the story of Daniel, how he rejected the rich food of Nebuchadnezzar's palace and ate only vegetables. The Bible says his beauty increased, and he advanced to the king's right hand, so how bad could it be?

But a curious thing happened. We noticed that Debby grew distant from the rest of the family. When we sat down to eat, talking and enjoying our meat and potatoes, she began to look down her nose at us—or so it seemed.

"Ugh, how can you eat that stuff?" she'd ask. "And think of the poor animal that had to be killed."

The rest of us shrugged it off, but it seemed to bother Debby more and more. And on the road it wasn't always easy for her to get vegetables to eat. This made her irritable and hard to live with sometimes.

You see what I'm getting at. We're back to the problem of attitude, and that does have spiritual implications. While Shirley and I were praying about that and living with it for a few long months, we noticed that there were also physical implications. Debby's normally beautiful blonde hair was becoming stringy and thin. She was mentioning it herself, though she hadn't made the connection between her hair and her diet. Also she was developing a skin problem and complaining that things looked blurry in front of her, and sometimes her eyes hurt.

"Alright, Deb!" I said one day. "I'm sorry, Honey, but we've gone as far as we can go with this vegetarianism. I'm your Daddy, and I've made a decision. I'm concerned about your physical health, and I'm now insisting that you start to eat some meat along with the vegetables."

Good ol' Deb; I love that girl! She had grown considerably since the "wallpaper days," and accepted what I said with grace. She wasn't happy about it, of course, but we'd been learning about the value of submission to authority. She knew the Lord would bless her if she did what I said. So she started with a little chicken and fish, and gradually would nibble at a lamb chop or a piece of beef. It did make her sick a few times, because the body does adjust to different eating habits in time. Now she's as healthy as a flea on a cat's back, eating a balanced diet, and looking more beautiful everyday!

Once in a while, both at home and on the road, I'll take turns sitting on the edge of the bed with one of the girls, having a chat. I like to encourage them when they're making an effort to do the right thing, and when they're not, I like to encourage them more. I reminded Deb a couple of times of Paul's admonition in Ephesians 6 (TLB): "Children, obey your parents; this is the right thing to do because God has placed them in authority over you.

"Honor your father and mother, this is the first of God's ten commandments that ends with a promise.

"And this is the promise: that if you honor your father and mother, yours will be a long life, full of blessing!"

And Debby sometimes reminded me of the next verse: "And now a word to you parents. Don't keep on scolding and nagging your children, making them angry and resentful. Rather, bring them up with the loving discipline the Lord Himself approves, with suggestions and godly advice."

You know, that's the only recipe for family togetherness, happy and well-rounded kids, and well-adjusted, confident parents.

Later on in Ephesians 6, Paul gives a sober warning about Satan's power and the weapons God gives us to withstand him. A lot of folks think that's just for "out in the world." Don't be fooled! The enemy of our souls hates the family worse than almost anything else in the world. It's a microcosm of heaven. It's a divine institution; it's where people have to love and laugh and give and grow.

So Paul's advice is absolutely essential—at home or on the road. Beginning to sound like church?

That's the next stop.

8

Glory, Glory, Ebenezer!

SHIRLEY & PAT

Pat: I'll explain this goofy-sounding title at the end of this chapter. Actually, it's appropriate.

Shirley: You're not talking about Ebenezer Scrooge, are you?

Pat: No, I'm talking about the hallelujahs that went up at our house when we finally found our church home. You remember all those long, gray days after we were disfellowshipped at our former church and the wilderness wandering when we weren't members anywhere?

Shirley: I sure do. We loved those folks at our former church and were active in the programs. There was a bustling young people's program and Sunday school classes for everybody. Our girls eagerly looked forward to their part in the classes, the services and in the social activities. There was a lot about that church that was fun. It was doctrinally sound, but there was a

79

sort of legalistic "uptightness" about it, a fear that we might "become like other people," and there was little teaching on life in the Spirit.

Pat: One morning in our adult Sunday school class, a deacon made this observation, "I work with a fine man every day, a Baptist. He's always talking about his love for the Lord, and I see him make difficult decisions that demonstrate his earnestness. He's moral, he's committed, and he's full of a bouncy joy. I feel guilty about not inviting him to come to church with me, but honestly, I don't think he'd enjoy it. He seems to be so happy where he is!"

I think most of us in the class appreciated his honesty. We felt the legal obligation to "convert" other people to our doctrinal positions, even when they seemed to have more of "the joy of the Lord" than we did!

Shirley: Another significant thing happened in the girls' Sunday school class. Several classes were combined because there was a guest teacher, a youth worker from across the country. He really had a way with kids. At one point in the class, he asked the fifty or sixty kids this question, "If Jesus were to come today, how many of you *know* that you'd go to heaven with Him?"

Only four kids raised their hands, and three of them were ours! Laury wasn't in that particular class, or her hand would have gone up too. Evidently, the rest of the kids just weren't sure of their salvation. I don't know what the elders thought of that, but it troubled Pat and me deeply. Certainly, Christians should know they're saved!

Pat: As I look back now, I feel our approach was this: do the best you can, and when you stand before God, He'll let you know if you passed or failed. You won't know until then. That's a tough way to live.

While all this was going on, and the handwriting was definitely on the wall (that we'd be moving elsewhere soon), Shirley's sisters were having problems in their Baptist church!

Shirley: Yes, Julie and Jennie, my married sisters, and their husbands and kids were also having their own personal encounters with the Holy Spirit and beginning to grow tremendously. They were active in one of the nation's largest Baptist churches in Van Nuys, California, but they were having problems just about like ours!

As they told their elders and other members about the miracles the Holy Spirit had done in their lives, they found they were "rocking the boat." Sunday school officers, and even the minister were calling them in for conferences.

Pat: Wasn't it one of your sisters who first told us about Church on the Way?

Shirley: Yes, Jennie and Julie and their families were visiting a church down the street from their Baptist church and were urging us to come with them. They were excited about the reality of worship there, the fact that the minister encouraged individuals to seek the Lord themselves and to bring their experiences to the worship times. It was almost the reverse of what we all were experiencing in our traditional churches. So one Sunday we went with them.

Pat: I'll never forget it. As my TV buddy, Jim Hampton, was to say later, "Don't go there unless you're really ready to make a decision about Jesus. Spectators don't last long at Church on the Way." After two or three times at that place, you know what's happening there is not phony.

Either you accept it and become involved and commit your life to the Lord—or walk away and never come back. It's not "church"; it's Jesus.

Our first Sunday there was a revelation. The building seemed small, but cheery. There were about eighty people, and they all really seemed to care about each other. The minister, Jack Hayford, had the most "unpreacherly" way about him, strolling up and down the aisles while he spoke, with absolutely no pretense and a great sense of humor. His grasp of the Word was impressive, but his commitment to the Lord stirred me even more.

There seemed to be no prearranged order for the service; there was lots of singing, almost never from a book, but from memory. A couple of times there was a message in tongues, followed immediately by an interpretation. Jack and the congregation took it all in stride. There was a real sense of the Lord's presence, and I think I wiped tears from my eyes several times.

Shirley: The part that moved me the most was the "prayer circle" time. We'd never experienced anything like that anywhere! Somewhere in the middle of the service, Jack Hayford encouraged all of us to make little circles of three or four and pray with each other about our specific and immediate needs. We found ourselves praying with people we'd never met until then, but who were concerned about each other's needs. It was so real, so right—so truly Christian.

We visited Church on the Way more and more. We kept open minds for a period of months. We were traveling a lot, too, so that stretched it out further.

Pat: But more and more, we knew where "home" was. Our girls were frightened, I think, that we might settle somewhere else! Never in my life, in over thirty years of faithful church attendance, had I been so eager to get to a worship service! And we wanted to take people with us.

The worship was always real. It was changing and growing, and it seemed that in each service the Lord spoke to us in some powerful and pointed way. And not just to us as a group, but to each of us as individuals —a personalized message.

That will explain why Church on the Way has grown from its original forty members, when Jack Hayford first "signed on" about seven years ago—to its present seven thousand or so regulars! Something's happening there!

Blacks and Chicanos, Orientals and Jews, Catholics and former agnostics—and lots of entertainer-type folks have all made it their church home. That's where Jim Hampton comes in.

Shirley: We've known Jim since we went to North Texas State together. Jim was cheerleader and campus clown. Jim and Pat were in the KA fraternity together.

Later Pat and I moved to New York, but we always stayed in touch with Jim. He was away in the army for a while, and then we introduced him to Carole, his wife-to-be. Eventually, we all moved west, and Jim is now doing great in television, movies and commercials.

For a while Jim wasn't interested in church or Christian things. He was too busy with his career, and he's always been a realist. Crazy, funny, but a realist.

Pat: We'd go to boxing matches and basketball games together, and really laugh it up. But when I'd talk about Jesus or the wonderful things the Holy Spirit was showing us, Jim would turn me off! One night I gave him a copy of *A New Song*, and he took it home to Carole. She read it and called Shirley. She wanted what we had.

Shirley: Soon Carole was baptized in the Holy Spirit, and there was a terrific change in her life. She didn't tell Jim about that, but she urged him to come to Church on the Way with her. And he did.

Pat: It really blew his mind! He enjoyed the singing and good-humored preaching. But when he heard a message in tongues, right away he thought to himself, *That's it. No more for me. I'm not ever coming to this church again.* And he meant it!

He admitted later, though, that when he heard that language, he knew it wasn't gibberish. He knew somehow that it was real. Then when the interpretation was given, he knew that was real too. Intuitively, he realized one was the interpretation of the other. (I guess that's why Paul says in I Corinthians 14 that tongues can be a sign to the unbeliever.) But, right then, it was just too much for Jim.

Shirley: Then a funny thing happened. A few nights later Jim's friend, Burt Reynolds, was putting on a big bash at his home. Carole knew it would be a fairly wild party and decided she didn't want to go. Besides it was on a Sunday night, and she wanted to go to church.

"Wouldn't you rather go to Church on the Way with me, Honey?" Carole asked.

"Nope, Babe, I'm not going there anymore. But you can if you want to. I understand, and it's alright with me. Burt's expecting me anyway."

Actually, Jim admitted to us later that he thought to himself, *I'll get half-crocked and have a good enough time that I can forget this Church on the Way stuff.*

But it didn't work that way.

Pat: After he got to the party, Burt asked him, "Where's Carole?"

Jim mumbled something about her being at church.

"What church?" Burt asked.

"Oh, you've never heard of it. It's called Church on the Way."

"*I've* heard of that church!" one of the other guests said, moving towards Jim. "Some of my best friends go there, and they're trying to explain it to me. What's going on there, anyway?"

Before he knew what was happening, Jim was surrounded by

most of the folks at the party, mainly Hollywood entertainers. The more he described the services, the attitude and the reality that he'd seen there, the more interested the other people became. After a while, Jim realized that he was running from something that most of these other people seemed to *want!* It shook him up.

He admits that he drank more than usual that night, but it didn't seem to affect him. He couldn't get drunk. He came home late after the party, and Carole was asleep. He woke her up.

"Alright," he said. "Tonight's the night. Either I get filled with the Holy Spirit like you, or we get a divorce."

"Well, Honey, you'd better call Jack Hayford," she said. It was after midnight, but Jim called him anyway.

"Come on over, Jim," Jack invited sleepily.

Jim was still highly agitated when he arrived at Jack's home. Wisely, Jack simply sat and listened while Jim poured out his venom on the church and on its influence over Carole. Finally, he stopped.

"Well, you realize the Holy Spirit is working on you right now, don't you?" Jack asked.

Jim thought about it a minute. "Yeah . . . I guess He is."

"Then it's just a matter of whether or not you want to be filled with the Holy Spirit."

"Okay, I do."

"Then let's ask the Lord to do it."

So Jack began to pray. But he hadn't prayed long before Jim interrupted him and began to confess his sins. When he finished, Jack urged him to ask the Lord to baptize him with the Holy Spirit, and Jim did.

Then Jack began to praise the Lord in his own prayer language, and Jim began a faltering attempt to do that too. In that moment God gave Jim an unusual prayer language! *Laughter!* First came a chuckle, then a ripple, then a guffaw, and finally ten or fifteen minutes of roaring, room-shaking, cascading, soul-shaking and heart-cleansing laughter! Jack

Hayford couldn't help joining in, and as the tears rolled down their cheeks, Jim found all kinds of new words forming and rippling out on the gales of joyous laughter.

The Lord knows us so well! And He treats us each so uniquely, so individually. He knew that Jim's stock in trade was laughter, that his special gift is making other people laugh. In Galatians 5:22 Paul specifically says that joy is one of the fruits of the Holy Spirit.

One of these days I want Jim to write his own story and fill in the special details. But his is just one example of what's going on at Church on the Way. To paraphrase the old TV show, "Naked City," Church on the Way has almost seven thousand stories. This is one of them.

Shirley: And you could add the stories of people like Dean Jones, Joanna Moore, Dorsey Burnett, Bob Goulet, Johnny Mann, Chuck Woolery and Joann Pflug, Tom Netherton—as well as screen writers, directors and producers, all kinds of folks in the entertainment business. None of them perfect, just forgiven and growing. Like the bumper sticker says, "Be patient; God's not finished with me yet."

We feel somehow that the Lord has made this congregation a "testing ground" for a new spiritual invasion of the entertainment world.

Pat: Yes, but it's not just happening at Church on the Way. The Holy Spirit is invading every church group that will let Him in!

My father, A.A. Boone, has been a Bible student and Sunday School teacher as long as I can remember, in Nashville. He has always gotten up at 5:00 or 5:30 to get his breakfast and read his Bible before beginning his day as a building contractor. He and Mamma took us to Sunday School before we were old enough to sit up! But they were worried when we told them about our baptism in the Holy Spirit.

"Son, I can tell something good has happened to you and

Shirley, but be careful; I've never believed that the things you're telling me are possible for our day. You know we've always taught that those things ceased in the first century. Sounds like you might be heading down a dangerous road."

Then, as he told us later, he went to work to "straighten us out." He looked up all the references to the Holy Spirit in the Bible, tried to build a real case for the "going out of the miracle business" in the first centruy. But the more he studied, the more he felt it was impossible to prove us wrong. Actually, his studies seemed to prove the *reverse:* that nowhere does the Bible say that the Holy Spirit will cease His supernatural and miraculous working with believers!

So he eventually decided, "Well, maybe Pat and Shirley are okay, but surely this is not for everybody."

But he kept on studying and discovered *he* was on a dangerous road, too! He saw that Peter on the day of Pentecost had said that "This promise is for *everybody*, as many as the Lord our God shall call!"

Now he had to decide whether he and Mamma *wanted it.* It was clear that Jesus had promised to all His disciples an exciting life filled with power and the evidence of God's supernatural working in daily situations. But let's face it, it's frightening to think about living a first century kind of life in today's world!

Still, Dad did his own investigating. He went to several Full Gospel Business Men's meetings, and was turned off. They seemed to be too emotional, at least in the meetings he attended, and there was an undue emphasis on speaking in tongues.

So he prayed, "Lord, fill me with Your Spirit. And if You want me to have any of these gifts of Your Spirit—that's fine, too. But I want them to be real, not forced or imagined. Just let me know they are from You."

Shirley: This is the kind of prayer I believe God delights to answer. We've seen it so many times. Especially people in the entertainment profession, who are constantly dealing with the unreal and the superficial; they have to work with make-believers, and they're leery of anything that appears to be "put-on" or just emotional. Daddy and Mamma are like that. They want to be sure, especially in a spiritual experience, that what they're experiencing is real and truly from God Himself.

Pat: So you can imagine our excitement one morning when Dad called me from Nashville. Mamma was on the phone with him.

"I was reading my Bible and praying this morning, Son," he told me. "It was just a regular morning, and I was thanking the Lord for all the good things He's done for Mamma and me, and especially what He's done for each of our children. As I prayed, I was filled with gratitude. There was a painful catch in my throat. I realize I've had that feeling many times before, and rather than choking back this feeling, as I've done before, I just let it out! From my mouth came this prayer language! It was quiet, just a relief to freely express my love and gratitude to the Lord, without having to grope self-consciously for the words. I wasn't speaking in English, but I *knew* I was telling the Lord exactly what I felt in my heart. It was beautiful."

Even over the phone, I could tell that Mamma was in tears.

"I'm so glad for Daddy, children. It hasn't happened for me, yet, but I'll just keep trusting the Lord. You all pray for us."

Shirley: We were all crying tears of joy. I knew that Pat's parents were not just looking for an experience. They really wanted to be filled with the Holy Spirit, so that the Lord could have His way with them more perfectly. And, of course, it happened. In just a few days God answered Mamma's prayer in a unique way.

She had a vivid dream in which Jesus was approaching her rapidly in the midst of a turbulent, cloud-filled sky. In her moment of recognition of Jesus as Lord, rivers of praise began to pour from her lips. This was in her dream, but when she awoke, she found that the praise was continuing! She was sitting up on bed, the tears coursing down her cheeks, while she worshipped our Jesus in a sweet and beautiful language of praise.

Pat: And soon after that, *they* were disfellowshipped from their church too. Dad's construction company had built this magnificent church building, and they still go there every Sunday morning and sit in the same place they have for years—but now as loving visitors, not members. Though he served that congregation as a deacon and Bible teacher for over thirty years, he's no longer considered a member because of his experience with the Holy Spirit.

Shirley: They also worship at The Lord's Chapel at least once every Sunday. That church started in a little house on the outskirts of Nashville. It has grown by leaps and bounds in just two or three years. They bought buildings, knocked out the walls, rebuilt and remodeled, and they can't build fast enough to contain their growth! And it's just because they have opened up to what the Lord wants to do with people—and with churches! They don't limit or hold Him back; they welcome His life among them.

And Mamma and Daddy are sharing that life all over the country now, telling what the Lord has done for them. Maybe they should write a book called *Life Begins at 70!*

Pat: Great idea, and they just may do it! Shall I explain the chapter title now?

Shirley: Yes, what in the world do you mean by "Glory Glory Ebenezer"?

Pat: Well, if you'll check in the first few chapters of I Samuel, you'll see a certain parallel between the Israelites' situation and ours. The Philistines defeated them and stole the Ark of the

Covenant—the manifestation of God's presence in their lives!

But God still loved them, and through no effort of their own, He caused the Philistines to give them back the Ark. Once again, they had the thrill of knowing that the Lord was in their midst! The prophet Samuel told them, "If you really want to return to the Lord, get rid of all your foreign gods and those religious things that you have made your idols. *Determine to obey only the Lord;* then He will rescue you from the Philistines" (I Samuel 7).

So the children of Israel did that, and there was even a great "water" ceremony. The Lord Jesus refers to the Holy Spirit as a baptism and a well of water. And then the Israelites were attacked again!

But this time the Lord gave them a mighty victory, working for them and through them. And it was then that Samuel "took a stone and placed it between Mizpah and Jeshanah and named it Ebenezer (meaning "the stone of help"). For he said 'the Lord has certainly helped us' " (I Samuel 7:12).

Shirley: Glory, glory, Ebenezer! The Lord *is* our stone, our rock, and He *has* helped us so wonderfully!

Pat: That's it. And you know how much we needed that "help" as we faced the new problems just ahead of us then.

9

Spiritual Gifts in Family Life

SHIRLEY

"Let love be your greatest aim; nevertheless, ask also for the special abilities the Holy Spirit gives, and especially the gift of prophecy, being able to preach the messages of God" (I Corinthians 14:1 TLB).

Did it ever occur to you this Scripture might apply to home life? I know Paul is talking mainly about church practice, but we've discovered you can take those "special abilities" home with you!

If you read the Bible much, it becomes crystal clear that supernatural gifts were operating freely in the first century church. What happened? Why did they quit? I don't know. Possibly because of confusion and misuse in some churches, or because of spiritual indifference. I have a hunch some Christian leaders thought they'd outgrown them.

But if you can put off doctrinal blinders and just accept the Bible for what it says, you must come to this conclusion: the Scripture not only lists gifts available to believers, but also says that we are to desire these gifts.

So in our family life we have asked the Lord to show us how to use these gifts which the Holy Spirit has given to members of God's family. After all, we are the church, whether we're in a special building or at home.

I don't say we've always used these gifts properly. I wouldn't even say that we have always used them when we needed them. But I can say that the Lord has proven His faithfulness as "the giver of every good and perfect gift," and showed Himself very near, tender and patient, involved in our immediate needs. Pat and each of the girls will tell you that submitting ourselves to the Holy Spirit and seeking these spiritual gifts has produced real growth in each of us and tremendous family unity.

I've been amazed at how ready our teenage girls were to trust the Holy Spirit after each received her baptism and prayer language. Sometimes they seemed to have more faith than Pat and I did—possibly because they didn't have to unlearn as much wrong doctrine!

Pat and I have already told in other books about special miracles of healing and other ways God answered specific prayers of our girls. You may have read "Miracle of the Mouse," in which God actually gave new life to Lindy's pet mouse as she and Pat prayed over it. This wasn't just for the sake of the mouse; it was a tremendous boost to Lindy's own faith.

You may have read of another time when a total stranger, a handsome, black man, came to our door and told Pat, "I don't know why I'm here. God has sent me, and I'm just waiting to find out why."

Pat had asked him to wait and gathered me, Laury and Cherry upstairs for prayer. We asked the Lord to reveal why this black man was on our front doorstep. As we prayed in the Spirit, the Lord showed Cherry that the man was "blinded by material things." Through Laury came this word: "He is being drawn into a cult."

Now to the best of our knowledge, Laury didn't even know

what the word *cult* meant. (She was only eleven.) But sure enough, as Pat and I spent time with this man and his wife, those two words of wisdom proved 100 percent correct.

There's a lot more to the story, but the happy ending is that Pat baptized the man and his family in our swimming pool. As far as we know, they're still following the Lord.

How can I describe the thrill of having the Lord instruct or bless us through our own children? Of hearing one daughter deliver a message in tongues and another give the interpretation in our family prayer time? And sometimes a word of knowledge or word of wisdom comes from our own child with profundity that couldn't *possibly* be her own.

One time the Lord had been nudging me about a word of wisdom or exhortation I had for Pat. But I was holding back; I thought he would not receive it from me. (It's hard for even a Spirit-filled husband to take instruction from his wife!) We were having our evening time of worship just before Cherry was to leave on a trip to Israel. We'd all expressed ourselves to the Lord, and I could sense that Pat was about to bring our time together to a close. I interrupted with a loud sigh.

Immediately, I came under conviction. *That really wasn't of the Lord,* I thought to myself.

"Do you think the Lord still has something to say to us, Honey?" Pat asked. Then he quickly added, "Well, let's wait before Him a little longer."

Suddenly, it seemed that the Lord got through to each of us, and we began to worship Him in a way we had not done together in a long time. Through first one girl and then another, operating in several spiritual gifts, we received real exhortation and instruction, particularly in regard to Cherry's upcoming trip.

But I didn't have the courage to let the Lord speak through me on the subject that He'd placed on my heart. So I asked the Lord to use one of the other girls.

"Perhaps Lindy, Lord," I said, since up until that time she

hadn't been exercising the gifts of the Spirit easily.

I leaned over to her, "Do you have a message from the Lord for us, Lindy?"

"No."

"Are you sure?"

She shook her head.

"Do you hear the Lord speaking to you, Lindy?" I asked.

Again she said no.

So I laid my hand on her head and said, "Lord God, You've created this universe; You spoke this earth into existence. Now please speak this message into Lindy's mind."

After a moment of further prayer, she looked at me, "Mama, do you know what it is?"

"Yes, that's why you must give it," I said.

Lindy has such a gentle disposition that I knew how difficult it would be. Yet in obedience to the Holy Spirit she told Pat that the Lord not only wanted him to serve as priest to his family, but also to be a prophet. He wanted Pat to speak His will to us.

Pat admitted that Lindy's prophetic message was "right on," and he needed it. We had slipped into a pattern in which the girls and I had felt prompted to give messages in tongues and interpretations, while Pat seemed content to act as "priest," to offer praise to the Lord and lead us in worship. Now the Lord wanted him also to exercise the gift of prophecy. As he had spoken to the Lord for us, now he should speak to us for the Lord. And none of us then could know how vital hearing from God through Pat would be in the days ahead.

As we've continued to exercise these gifts in our family worship, there have been tremendous physical blessings, too!

On one occasion we were performing at the Playboy Hotel in New Jersey. We had really prayed for the Lord's guidance before accepting this engagement. And when we arrived at the hotel, we had a strong sense that we were like Daniel in the lion's den—in an atmosphere which could destroy us unless the Lord was truly with us. But we knew He was, because we were there to minister life in Jesus' name!

We had barely settled into our room when Lindy came down with a vicious attack of the flu, accompanied by laryngitis. She could hardly make a sound, much less sing. We had two shows that night, so we prayed immediately for her. But Pat and I both had to admit that our faith was not strong. We were under intense pressure, and the need was urgent. We called a doctor.

Before the doctor could arrive, there was a knock at the door. Pat opened it to confront two young men with long hair.

"We believe the Lord has sent us to you," they said.

I couldn't understand how it had been possible for them to have gotten up to our room. The Playboy Hotel complex is under heavy security guard, and you have to show a membership card to even get in!

"Fellows, you'll just have to wait," Pat said. "We've got a real crisis here. My daughter has the flu and we've called for the doctor."

"That's why we're here," said one fellow. "We didn't know exactly what the problem was, but the Lord sent us."

"Well, okay, then come on in and join us in praying for Lindy," Pat said.

They joined us at Lindy's bedside, praising the Lord and praying for her healing. After a few minutes they left. Then the doctor arrived and examined her.

"There's no way this young lady is going to sing tonight," he said. "I'll give her a shot and some other medicine, but it will take two or three days before she'll be well enough to sing."

After the doctor left, we had dinner sent to the room and talked over the evening's performance. Lindy had hot soup.

As we got ready to do the show, she still didn't have much voice but she said, "I really believe that everything is going to be okay."

So we started the show. And in everything Lindy had to sing, *even in her solo part,* her voice was full and sure! It was truly a miracle!

How did those two fellows know where to find us? How did

they even get into the Playboy Hotel and up to our room? We don't know. We *do* know that the God of all power, grace and love ministered to Lindy through people we still don't know by name!

And then there are the gifts of wisdom and knowledge.

"For to one is given the word of wisdom through the Spirit, and to another the word of knowledge according to the same Spirit" (I Corinthians 12:8 NASB).

The Living Bible says it this way: "To one person the Spirit gives the ability to give wise advice; someone else may be especially good at studying and teaching, and this is his gift from the same Spirit."

My family had just returned from an extensive trip through the Orient, singing and sharing, and now the girls were plunged back into school work. Most of the teachers had given the girls assignments ahead of time, so they could keep up with their studies while we were traveling. That seemed to work well for everybody but Debby.

Poor Deb! At that point in her life, she wasn't the greatest of students and was still having personality problems with her teachers. One teacher had assigned an examination for the next day after we returned home, and Debby felt she wasn't ready for it. She begged me to write the teacher for an extension of time for her.

"Honey," Pat asked Debby, "I saw you studying this material all along the way, on the planes and in the hotel rooms. Didn't you complete all the assignments? Haven't you studied all of it?"

Debby said that she had, "But, Daddy, I'm just not ready to take an examination. I need more time; I know this will be a hard test, and I'll flunk it." She began to cry.

I looked at Pat. He was having a struggle. He wanted Debby to have more self-confidence, and he knew that she had studied the material. He didn't really feel he had the right to ask for more concessions from the school. I felt he was praying for wisdom. I know *I* was!

(Front, left to right) Cherry, Pat, Lindy. (In tree, left to right) Laury, Shirley, Debby.

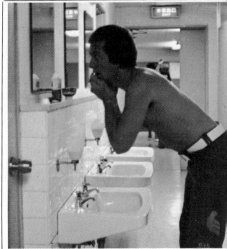

(Above) On the road—a succession of public restrooms, squinting bleary-eyed while scraping off that morning stubble.

(Left) "The Jolly Green Groaner"

The Boone family does the "Light Fantastic" in Syracuse, N.Y.

Billy Graham poses with Shirley and Pat at a tribute dinner for the evangelist in Los Angeles.

Cherry, Pat, Shirley, Lindy and Laury sit on a mountain top in the High Sierras in 1953.

In the film, The Cross and the Switch-blade, Pat plays Dave Wilkerson in a confrontation with Erik Estrada.

The Boone girls do a TV special by the Sea of Galilee.

Yaaa-a-ah!! A Boone family smile for the photographer.

Pat and Shirley demonstrate an ancient family custom.

Boones and balloons—the girls on an outing.

The first to become a bride, Cherry poses with her husband, Dan O'Neill, the Reverend Jack Hayford, and the bridal party.

Pat drives the get-away car.

Supporting Republican candidates, Pat meets with Mike Curb (left), California Republican Committee Chairman, former U.S. Senator George Murphy, and Margaret Brock, also active in Republican politics.

The Boones pose beside a wishing well in West Bend, Wisconsin, where they were doing commercials for the West Bend Company.

Lindy and Doug Corbin present Pat and Shirley with their first grandson—Ryan.

Pat chats with Bill Banowski, president of Pepperdine University, and Nobel prize winner Milton Friedman at a testimonial dinner for Friedman.

After long minutes of deliberation, Pat made up his mind.

"Debby, we'll all pray with you about it tonight before we go to bed. We've asked for all the extensions of time we can from the school. You've studied the material, and I know you have the brainpower to make a good grade. Now we're going to ask the Lord to bring it to your remembrance and help you to do well in this test."

We prayed that night, but Debby cried some more, because she really couldn't believe she'd be ready to take that test. The next morning she went bravely off to school to "face the music."

A couple of nights later at the dinner table, Debby came in after the rest of us had already started. As she sat down, and picked up her fork, we all sensed that something was up. She looked at her plate for a minute, then spoke in a subdued voice.

"Daddy, you know you told me to take that test when I knew I wasn't ready for it. . . ."

"Yes, Deb," Pat replied.

I'm sure he had the same fluttering in the stomach that I did. I thought to myself, *Oh no, have we pushed Debby too hard and further reinforced her feeling of inadequacy at school?*

"Well, I guess you'll be happy to know . . .," she paused for a long second, and then looked at Pat beaming, "I made an *A* on it."

All of us erupted into a chorus of whoops and howls and "praise the Lord's." I'm surprised we didn't turn the table over!

When the din subsided, Debby went on, "It was just amazing; I could hardly believe that the teacher was asking just the questions I knew the answers to!"

Some people may feel these weren't very urgent situations. But I'm sure that most caring, concerned mothers will identify with me and be grateful that the Lord is concerned about the inner workings of the family and the day-to-day problems of each of the kids. In this case, the Lord gave Pat the gift of wisdom: The priest-prophet in our house was able to give wise advice to his daughter in a tough (for her) situation. Then God gave, by His Spirit, the gift of knowledge to Debby. In spite of the intense pressure she was feeling, she knew the answers to all the questions. It appeared that the Lord had been preparing her for this while we traveled, since she just "happened" to study all the right things!

Paul sums it up this way: "Now there are varieties of gifts, but the same Spirit. And there are varieties of ministries, and the same Lord. And there are varieties of effects, but the same God who works all things in all persons. But to each one is given the manifestation of the Spirit for the common good!"

So many times the Lord has shown us that these gifts of His Spirit are for the family of God, and our own individual families as well. What marvelous blessings in the confused, complex, contradictory world we all live in!

Do they always work? No. I would be untruthful if I said that we've had supernatural answers to all our problems. Lots of times we've failed to ask; other times the Lord has chosen to let us muddle through on our own. I don't believe that He will give us specific answers to every problem we face. He wants us to apply the principles!

I hope this doesn't sound like we're promoting the gifts of the Holy Spirit for their own sake. That's the last thing we want to do. But we do want to share the value of allowing the Holy Spirit to work through family members who worship the Giver of the gifts. We're praying that the Lord will help us keep everything in balance.

We know that the greatest gift of all is Jesus Himself. Luke 10 tells that when His disciples returned from their first experience as channels of the Holy Spirit's power, Jesus cautioned them, "Behold, I have given you authority to tread upon serpents and scorpions, and over all the power of the enemy, and nothing shall injure you. Nevertheless, do not rejoice in this, that the spirits are subject to you, but rejoice that your names are recorded in heaven" (NASB).

But in countless precious ways, He's shown us that He is

always near, always ready to be involved with our family life. Sometimes, He'll even give us graduate courses—like He did with Pat in the financial area. My husband *did* finally graduate, and I want him to tell you what he learned.

10

Meanwhile, Back at the Cash Register

PAT

Whether your name is Rockefeller or Vanderbilt, Rothchild, Jones, or Boone—the Lord can teach you valuable lessons through money! I know—because He is still teaching me.

So much of His teaching centers around material things, money and possessions, and the way people use or misuse those things. In the Sermon on the Mount in Matthew 5-7 He talked about attitudes toward material things and money, "You cannot serve two masters; God and money. For you will hate one and love the other, or else the other way around."

Then He goes on to say, "So my counsel is: don't worry about things—food, drink, and clothes!"

But how can a husband and father *not* worry about his income, about money for clothes and school and hospitalization and insurance and all those bills?

He has to, doesn't he?

I wish I were a "super saint," and could tell you that I don't worry about all those things—but I really can't. I'm learning though. I'm seeing that we have to be concerned about earning a living, but the Lord doesn't want us to *worry*.

In fact,—He commands, "Be anxious in nothing." It's a *principle* that has to be learned and applied. And that takes experience.

That's why I'm telling you about the financial knotholes through which I was dragged. Through many a tight squeeze I've learned lessons and started applying principles, with amazing results!

I've always been such an optimist, a "possibility thinker," ready to invest and believe in other people's ideas. At one time I was involved in *thirty different businesses!* I was making so much money in entertainment that if a few of those businesses failed, it wasn't going to affect me seriously. I gave time, money and my name to a great many things, and firmly believed they would all succeed.

They didn't. During the severest spiritual testing time of our lives, these businesses began failing. Like a row of dominoes—click, click, click—they went down, one right after the other. There were fast-food franchise outfits, oil drilling ventures, TV repair companies, direct mail film developing plans, discount stores, all kinds of things! I believed in the people, I believed in the concepts, and I believed in just about everything but the Lord's will for my life!

Finally, at the end of the domino line, came the Oakland Oaks basketball collapse and the Wendell West Real Estate disaster. These things were so enormous that it appeared I was virtually wiped out.

And that's when I finally began to listen to the Lord and learn His lessons. "The love of money is the root of all evil" (I Timothy 6:10 KJV). I hadn't thought that I loved money, especially since I already had as much as a normal person would want. But I saw now I had become preoccupied with the thought of stacking up more of it!

So, at the very bottom of our financial valley, I went to my accountant.

"John," I said, "from now on I want you to take ten cents

out of each dollar that comes to me and put it in the Pat Boone Foundation."

This is a nonprofit foundation through which Shirley and I distribute our tithes and offerings to various ministries and Bible programs. It goes out just as fast as I can put it in—and sometimes faster!

"But you can't afford that, Pat," John cautioned. "Not right now!"

"John, I can't afford *not* to."

It was obvious to me that the troubles were so desperate that only the Lord could get me out of them, and I knew that He expected some kind of faith-action from me. In the third chapter of Malachi God says, *"You have robbed Me of the tithes and* offerings due to Me. And so the awesome curse of God is cursing you, for your whole nation has been robbing Me. Bring all the tithes into the storehouse so that there will be food enough in my Temple; if you do, *I will open up the windows of heaven for you and pour out a blessing so great you won't have room enough to take it in!"*

And just in case you're thinking that promise was only for the children of Israel under the old covenant, listen to Jesus: "For if you give, you will get! Your gift will return to you in full and overflowing measure, pressed down, shaken together to make room for more, and running over. Whatever measure you use to give, large or small, will be used to measure what is given back to you" (Luke 6:36-38 TLB).

I *had* to trust the Lord; I had no choice, really. I knew I couldn't solve my own problems. So I had to demonstrate my faith in Him, and I began to do it. That was the beginning of Financial Principle Number 1: *give, and it shall be given unto you.* I'll tell you how it turned out in just a moment.

But while I was thinking of giving, I also thought of forgiving. I couldn't avoid it. Again in the Sermon on the Mount, Jesus had said, "But if you do not forgive men, then your Father will not forgive your transgressions." I had committed all kinds of transgressions, including financial ones, and I needed the Lord's forgiveness and healing. Somehow He tied that in with my forgiveness of others!

Shirley and I felt the Lord speaking to us more specifically through the parable Jesus told in Matthew 18 (TLB). In this account a servant was forgiven a ten million dollar debt by the king. The servant turned around and imprisoned a man who owed him $2,000. Jesus has the king speak to the unforgiving servant this way: " 'You evil-hearted wretch! Here I forgave you all that tremendous debt, just because you asked me to—shouldn't you have mercy on others, just as I had mercy on you?'

"Then the angry king sent the man to the torture chamber until he had paid every last penny due. *So shall my Heavenly Father do to you* if you refuse to truly forgive your brothers."

Sort of hard to miss the point, isn't it?

Well, Shirley and I realized what we needed to do in obedience to that scriptural principle. As an aftermath of the Oakland Oaks situation, my former partner in that debacle had given me a personally signed note, obligating himself to pay me something over a million dollars! He didn't have the money, and there was no foreseeable way that he ever would. But it seemed good business for me to have such a note—in case he ever would be able to pay it.

Suddenly, tearfully, I identified completely with him. I really hadn't forgiven him either the financial or the moral debt of that situation. He was still being tortured by his debt to me, and I was being tortured by my debt to the Lord.

The picture was so clear to me. But when I told my accountant and lawyer what I was going to do, they were aghast.

"You can't do that!" they said. "You're already under a tremendous financial burden yourself. You can't afford to give away a million dollar asset, no matter how questionable it might be."

From a human standpoint they were right, of course. But because I was insistent, they prepared the papers. Then I invited my good brother to the house, and we sat down together. Shirley was with us.

"We realize that technically you owe us over a million dollars," I said. "But we got into that whole mess together with our eyes open and not really by the Lord's leading. We know that you really can't pay us this money, so we want to just tear up the papers. Brother, we forgive you this indebtedness."

It was an emotional moment for the three of us. He knew full well the principle we were employing, and he accepted the papers I handed him, which included his personal note to us. And I'm telling you, the love and forgiveness and reconciliation that flowed between us that day was worth more than any million dollars!

What happened after that? You guessed it!

At the end of the first year of our renewed tithing, in the midst of all of our problems, our accountant, John, shook his head.

"You know, Pat, it's been an amazing year. You haven't had a hit record; you haven't made a movie; your career has not apparently been in high gear, but your income has been high. And in spite of your giving 10 percent of your gross, you've made real progress on your indebtedness."

"John," I answered, "not in spite of—because of!"

John smiled and answered, "Maybe you've got something there. We've put 10 percent of your gross income in the foundation, and you've had very high expenses. Yet we've been able to meet all the expenses and all the loan commitments, pay all your taxes, and even put a little bit away. I really don't know how we've done it, and I'm your accountant!"

I laughed out loud now. I love John, and we've been learning these things together. "I think we've had some help from the Head Accountant, John!"

And the same thing has happened each year since!

Since then I have told lots of people, "I'm in a giving contest with the Lord—and I'm losing!" I recommend it to everybody!

Shirley's had her own personal experiences with this principle too. When she received the royalties from her own book, *One Woman's Liberation*, she figured that she could use those to help relieve our financial situation. But in prayer and study of the Word, the Lord showed her He hadn't inspired her to write a book to pay off our debts. So she wound up giving 90 percent of her royalties back to the Lord and keeping 10 percent for herself! Is it any wonder that the Lord has used her book so greatly?

Each of our girls has applied the same principles, and scrupulously tithes on every dollar she makes—even if it comes from me, and I've already tithed on it! You can't outgive God!

I still get letters which grieve me deeply. They come from people in every walk of life with financial problems and from investors in projects I once lent my name to. The second category causes me special heartache, because I can't help feeling partly responsible. And yet I've learned that I cannot be the solution to their problems. Only the Lord can.

I've nearly gotten ulcers worrying about the elderly school teachers, retired bank clerks and college kids who invested in real estate with me in more than one venture. It's taken many hours, on more than one occasion for my lawyer and accountant to help me see that I could not personally compensate one investor—without being liable for all of them. The human desire to play God has been almost irresistible because I fully sympathize with the grief over bad investments. I've been there!

But instead, I've had to write many long letters, sharing what I've learned from the Lord with these dear people, and urging them to look to Him as their solution. We all have to count on God's promise in Romans 8:28, "For *all things* work together for good to those who love the Lord, and are called according to His purpose." Even the setbacks. Even the losses. Even the heartbreak and disappointment. They're all lessons, if you'll allow them to be.

I've learned to be more cautious and have asked the Lord to make me a better steward. I never wanted to be like that one-talent man who was so afraid of doing something wrong that he did nothing. So I've usually gone to the other extreme and tried to do it all! Both extremes are wrong, and I'm trying to learn the balance between them.

It's very important that I do. After all, Jesus told His disciples, " 'Truly I say to you, it is hard for a rich man to enter the kingdom of heaven. And again I say to you, it is easier for a camel to go through the eye of a needle, than for a rich man to enter the kingdom of God.'

"And when the disciples heard this, they were very astonished and said, 'Then who can be saved?'

"And looking upon them Jesus said to them, 'With men this is impossible, but with God all things are possible' " (Matthew 19:23-26 NASB).

Evidently it's possible but only with the constant help of God!

Earlier in that same passage, Jesus said to the rich young ruler, "If you wish to be complete, go and sell your possessions and give to the poor, and you shall have treasure in heaven; and come, follow Me."

Lots of people, especially skeptical and cynical interviewers, have asked me why I didn't take that advice, if "you're such a good Christian"?

Shirley and I had to consider that too. Let us tell you how.

11
Channel of Blessing
or Empty Ditch

SHIRLEY & PAT

Shirley: I guess few things have wounded you more than that article in *Esquire,* have they, Honey?

Pat: No, that was a real blow to the solar plexus, an expert hatchet job. The writer of the article called me from New York, assured me he wanted to do an objective article on the Jesus movement, and asked for my help. I spent the better part of three days with him, taking him to baptisms at the beach, worship services, and even including him at a baptismal service at our pool here. He was taking notes constantly and appeared to be sympathetic and interested.

Then the article came out with a warped sort of drawing of me with my arms draped over my Rolls convertible. The title was "Pat Boone; What a Friend He Has in Jesus."

Throughout the article the writer implied that my involvement with the Jesus movement was some kind of money-making gimmick. He went to great pains to describe our house, all of our possessions, and mentioned my Rolls convertible several times. He completely ignored the fact that all these material things were the result of almost twenty years of success as an entertainer. I'd had all those things before I became involved in the Holy Spirit renewal. Though I had made it plain that there was nothing commercial about my commitment to Jesus, the writer didn't seem to hear me.

Shirley: I remember him asking you about the rich young ruler in the Bible, and why don't you sell everything you have and give it to the poor?

Pat: Yes, and he wasn't the only one. Writers from *McCall's,* the *Rolling Stone,* and a lot of other magazines, including *Fortune,* the businessmen's bible, confronted me with the same question.

Shirley: Didn't you get the feeling they were trying to put you on the spot, perhaps embarrass you and make you seem hypocritical?

Pat: Almost every time it was clear that the writer hoped I would do a little crawfish number and make some lame excuse for holding on to our possessions.

Every time I'd read them Mark 10:28-30 (NASB): "Peter began to say to Him, 'Behold, we have left everything and followed You.'

"Jesus said, 'Truly I say to you, there is no one who has left house or brothers or sisters or mother or father or children or farms, for My sake and for the Gospel's sake, but that *he shall receive a hundred times as much now in the present age,* houses and brothers and sisters and mothers and children and farms, along with persecution; and in the world to come, eternal life.'"

This is in the same chapter as Mark's account of the rich young ruler! It's clear to me that the Lord rewards those who give up *anything* to follow Him! And He rewards them materially!

Shirley: And then there's that little three-word warning, "along with persecutions." That always scared me, mainly because I didn't understand it.

Pat: I didn't either, so when you started suggesting that we put our house and cars and everything up for sale, I thought you might be right. We were still having financial problems, and it seemed to both of us that the Lord might want us to do that.

Shirley: I felt that perhaps we weren't sacrificing enough. So I let our cook go, and I started doing all the meals and a lot of the housekeeping myself.

Pat: And with us on the road, you had to learn songs and take care of the girls' wardrobe along with all your other responsibilities. This was a real hardship on you, wasn't it.

Shirley: Well, yes, but that's not the point. I felt that if people were criticizing us and doubting our commitment to the Lord because of our material possessions, maybe we should sell some things. Perhaps this would prove to the Lord and to other people that we were "good Christians," or at least trying to be sincere.

I realize now that on my part a lot of this was pride and unwillingness to face criticism. I was starting to behave like the "one-talent man" who hid his abilities under a rock for fear of misusing them.

Pat: I plead guilty too. Remember my effort to sell the Rolls? That car had been a dream come true to me. It's a beautiful Rolls convertible that I had painted white and chocolate brown—the prettiest thing on four wheels I've ever seen! I really loved it, and still do.

I thought to myself, *maybe that's the trouble. Maybe you*

love it too much; maybe the Lord wants you to give it up.

I knew that selling the car would not really affect our financial situation, because our problems were so big. But if selling that car would please the Lord and remove a stumbling block for other people, I ought to do it.

So I prayed this way, "Lord, You gave me that car. You know how much I've loved it, and I thank You for it. Now I'm willing to give it up if that will please You. I'm sending it in to be serviced where other Rolls owners can see it. Lord, if I should sell it, will You just have someone offer me what I have in it? I know it's worth a good bit more now, but if someone offers me just what I have invested in it, I'll sell it and know that I have heard Your voice."

I trembled a little as I uttered that prayer because I fully expected the Lord to take me up on it.

Shirley: And I loved you for it, because I knew how much that car meant to you. I really expected that someone would offer you just the right price.

Pat: But it didn't happen! I purposely let the car stay at the dealer's for almost three weeks. Every time the phone rang, I was sure it was someone wanting to buy my convertible. But there wasn't a nibble.

Shirley: Wait a minute, there was that fellow who wrote you from Florida, remember? Out of the blue you got this letter saying, "I hear you want to sell your prestige car." You thought that was "it," didn't you?

Pat: That's right. I had forgotten. And the guy even asked me to send him some Polaroid pictures! So I took some. To my great dismay, they turned out beautifully! They made the car look like Solomon's chariot—irresistible to anyone interested in a Rolls Royce convertible.

My heart was in my white bucks as I mailed those pictures

off. I figured it was "good-by, drop-top!" But I never heard from the man again!

Shirley: No, eventually, even I was able to see that this was simply a test from the Lord. He wanted you to prove that you were willing to give it up. And then He let you keep it! We went through the same thing with our house.

Pat: That was a *real* test. The Lord gave us this house, right smack in the heart of Beverly Hills in 1960. We've raised our family here, opened the doors for Bible studies and worship times, and baptized over three hundred people in our swimming pool. It's home, and who wants to sell his home?

Still, more than once, we've spoken to the Lord this way: "Lord God, You gave us this house. And now we give it back to You. We've loved living here, and we've loved having You live with us here. But if it would please You for us to sell it, just send someone to us who wants to give us what it's worth."

Shirley: And real estate people gave us appraisals. We let them know that if someone wants to buy our house for its current appraised price (with just a little more added as a sure sign from the Lord), we'll sell it and move on. Like real estate everywhere, the value has gone up a great deal in the last seventeen years.

But so far that person hasn't come. And until he does, Pat and I and the girls live here rejoicing and thanking the Lord every day!

Pat: I believe there's a lesson in this. Jesus *did* require that rich young ruler to sell *his* possessions and give them to the poor. The young ruler walked away sorrowfully, because he wasn't willing to do what Jesus asked. Jesus had seen that weakness in him and, therefore, had given him a special command.

I don't believe He asks each of us to do that. But He does

want each of us to be willing to do it. The *love* of money is the root of all evil, not the money itself.

When Jesus says, "Give and it shall be given to you," He wants us to learn and practice a principle. I earnestly believe that God wants every one of His children to prosper. He wants us to own things, but things should not own us.

He wants to make us channels of blessing, not empty ditches. Once we learn how to use and give material things, I think He wants to entrust them to us. He says through Paul, "If a man will judge himself, he will not need to be judged."

So we keep saying, "Lord, how are we doing in this area? Is it okay? Do You mind if I keep this or that? If not, You can have it."

We're learning the joys of giving and looking for opportunities to give more. We are seeking the Lord's counsel and direction in that too!

Shirley: When you read the Bible, it's hard to miss the fact that God gave Abraham, Isaac, David, Solomon and so many of His servants tremendous material blessings. And they were constantly thanking Him, acknowledging His goodness publicly, and then looking for ways to bless others.

Whenever they failed to do that, they had problems. And that's where those three little words, "along with persecutions," come in! We have seen that the Lord *must* accompany material blessings with various kinds of tests and challenges, so that the one receiving the blessings must constantly trust the Lord, not material things. Nothing will accomplish that like persecutions.

Pat: Right. The Lord wants us to know what it's like to be children of the King. He says, "If you're faithful in a few things, I'll make you ruler over much!" That's His desire for all of us. And the love of money (the root of all evil) is no more prevalent among well-to-do people than among those who don't have much. In fact, it seems to me that, with obvious notable exceptions, the less people have, the more they are likely to love money. Maybe that's why Jesus spent so much time talking to the "have-nots" about material things.

Like Paul, we've learned both to be abased and to abound—to be poor or to be rich. We've been both places, and we've learned why persecutions accompany material things— we *need* the problems to keep us in line and to keep our eyes on the Lord. Then we are better prepared to receive the promises.

Shirley: And the problems sure keep coming, don't they? You've had loans called in unexpectedly, tax rulings that went against you, even after you'd paid lots of money for good legal and tax advice. And that judgment against you involving the Oakland Oaks.

Pat: Yeah, that was a rough one. Because again my reputation suffered, as well as my finances. But in this case, I think I deserved it. Frank Mieuli of the San Francisco Warriors demanded and got a million dollar judgment against me for persuading Rick Barry to play basketball for the Oakland Oaks. Barry had been the star forward of Mieuli's Warriors, and my partner and I had persuaded him to come play for us, giving him a chunk of the franchise. Well, several years went by. Rick played for a couple of ABA teams, then went back to the Warriors. But Frank Mieuli still pressed his claim.

One day I flew up to San Francisco with my lawyers to see him. We were seeking an out-of-court settlement. After a long discussion we saw we weren't getting any place. I asked to talk to Franklin alone.

"Franklin, I was wrong," I said. "I couldn't really say this in front of the lawyers for legal reasons, but I want you to know that I had an ethical and moral lapse several years ago.

"My lawyers then were advising me I was within my right, but I was overlooking Rick Barry's moral responsibility to finish his contract with you. I thought I was right then, but I wasn't. I want you to forgive me. If I had the kind of money you're asking for, I would give it to you, but I don't."

This didn't seem to go very far with Mr. Mieuli. He let me know in no uncertain terms that he intended to get that judgment in court.

"I want to let the world know that the white bucks, all-American-kid is wrong and this scruffy, little Italian is right! I don't want your apologies, I don't want your settlement offer. I want a million dollar judgment. And I'm going to get it!" he said.

And he did! I'm still paying off that settlement in annual installments, and since then I've sent Franklin The Living Bible with his name on it, my own book *A New Song*, and several personal letters letting him know that I feel God's will has been done. I am glad that he and the Warriors and Rick Barry are doing so well, and I figure I just learned some high-priced lessons.

Shirley: Very high-priced lessons!

Pat: I've laughed about it a lot since the pain died down. Looking back, I realize that my involvement with the Oakland Oaks cost me something over two million dollars—and I only saw ten games! I had good seats alright, but they were hardly worth $200,000 a ticket.

Shirley: Since then we've been learning to consult the Lord about everything, whether professional, financial, spiritual or whatever. We've learned that *everything* God has created is for our good and is intertwined with everything else. We don't try to separate the spiritual from the material any more. Paul says, "You have everything when you have Christ, and you are filled with God through your union with Christ" (Colossians 2:10 TLB).

The Lord uses everything to teach us how to serve Him better. We're not going to sell or give away what we have to please other people, or to avoid criticism. But if the Lord *directs* us to do those things, I pray we'll have the willingness and the sensitivity to do it. We trust Him that much.

Pat: In our own way we've offered it all to God anyway. In our desire to serve the Lord, and in real concern for a sick and dying world all around us, we've done some quite "uncommercial" things. We've spoken about Christ freely and boldly on television; written articles in all kinds of magazines; told our story in books, on television and in person all over the country—and in the opinion of our public relations people and some of our agents, thus have committed professional suicide.

We've risked everything we have on the proposition that God Himself will provide for us if we live for Jesus and for the Gospel, the "good news" that God loves us all enough to have died for us!

Shirley: And it's really remarkable what's happened. When TV and movie opportunities closed up, partly because of our Christian beliefs, other doors opened! People even came from Japan to ask us to do commercials for them!

Pat: Yes, they asked "Mr. Milk" to do commercials for Maxwell House coffee in Japan! Milk isn't so plentiful there, and I knew about their huge alcohol consumption. I figured coffee would be a pretty good antidote, so Shirley and the girls and I did some beautiful commercials that really sold the coffee in Japan! They gave us credit for selling forty or fifty million dollars worth in a couple of years. Folks from Brazil were starting to cry, "Enough!"

Shirley: We really needed the money, but the best part is we put a spiritual message in the commercials! Since none of us could speak Japanese, the Japanese wrote a song for Pat to record. It played through the whole one-minute commercial.

The words had to do with the blessings of family life and how good it is to "thank God every day"! This really isn't a Buddhist concept; they wrote that because they knew it's something *we* would want to say! Praise the Lord!

Pat: And there was the time several years ago when I knew the Lord had commissioned me to write a couple of books. One was *A Miracle a Day Keeps the Devil Away,* about the many miracles the Lord had performed in our daily lives. The other was *Dr. Balaam's Talking Mule,* about the divisions in the church.

I knew I had to write both books and that they would be time-consuming. I also had to pay our bills, so I asked the Lord, "Father, will You supply the necessary finances in some quick way, so that I can take the time to write these books?"

I figured that if the commission was real, the Lord would supply the means. And He did it! I was approached to do a commercial for Jockey T-shirts. It was a silly little thing where I sang about "white is right" with three teenage guys behind me singing about the joys of brightly colored undershirts. It was a good product and a funny commercial. I don't know if it sold Jocky T-shirts, but it provided enough money for me to write those books.

Shirley: We've learned so much through all of this. III John 2 says, "Beloved, I pray that in all respects *you may prosper* and be in good health, just as your soul prospers" (NASB). I Corinthians 16:2 admonishes, "On the first day of every week let each one of you put aside and save, *as he may prosper"* (NASB).

I get the message that God really wants us to prosper, materially and physically, and that these things are directly related to our spiritual growth.

Pat: Honey, I think you've hit it right on the head. Solomon, the wealthiest man who ever lived, and perhaps the wisest, said, "The generous man will be prosperous, and he who waters will himself be watered" (Proverbs 11:25 NASB).

Jesus put it this way: "Seek *first* the kingdom of God—and all these *things* will be added to you." We've learned that God uses material things to teach us spiritual principles. He wants us to learn to trust Him completely and to love and care for each other.

Shirley: It's taken some real hard knocks for me to learn how to trust God—and even harder ones to teach me to trust my husband!

12

Blowouts on the Road

SHIRLEY

Ever watch the "Partridge Family" on TV? With four teenage girls in our house, you can bet we did. Lots of times. In case you've forgotten, Shirley Jones and David Cassidy starred with a group of attractive young people. It concerned a mother, her singing kids, and the mom's efforts to keep her family going while they sang for a living!

We always felt it was *our* story. The only difference was that we didn't always get our problems solved in a half hour! Not by a long shot. The pressures of packing and unpacking, planes and hotels and dressing rooms, rehearsals and shows and late nights and weather-grounded planes, and chartered bus breakdowns—with four teenage girls—are almost indescribable.

I always chuckled at the way Shirley Jones and the Partridge family seemed to sail through, laughing and happy, with an absolute minimum of friction between members. It seemed so wonderful, so desirable and yet it was never that simple for us. And if Pat and I hadn't always been demanding and concerned parents, things could have been a lot worse!

One time Merv Griffin had us all on his TV show. After he

had talked to Pat and me for a while, he asked, "Can I talk to the girls without you butting in? They *do* talk for themselves, don't they?"

We laughed and assured him they did.

So he asked, "Aren't your mom and dad pretty strict parents—especially by Hollywood standards?"

"Oh, yes," they said.

"What are they strictest about?" he asked.

"Respect," Cherry said.

And the audience applauded!

We have always demanded respect. We've felt we were friends to our daughters, but that we had to be much more than that. We knew they'd have many friends but only one mother and father. We've never let them forget that.

But Merv Griffin didn't let it end there.

"Now, be honest with me," he probed. "Hasn't having strict parents caused you to miss out on some things?"

And one of the girls shot back, "Oh, yes—*trouble.*"

Again the audience applauded. Then the girls went on to explain. They said they were grateful that we had been protective and strict because this had helped them avoid the pitfalls some of their friends had encountered. And they even indicated that more than one of their friends was envious of our concerned attitudes. The friends wished *their* parents would be more strict sometimes.

You see, we've discovered that loving discipline is one very important way of letting your kids know you really care about them. It's not easy, and they don't like it at the moment, but in time they come to appreciate it.

Naturally, discipline is not enough. Our family has stayed so close that our girls have seen our imperfections clearly and have learned to accept us just as they do each other. In other words, we make mistakes just as they do. But we *are* their parents, and we have the God-given responsibility to point out their mistakes and help them avoid repeating them.

Sometimes the reverse is true! I'm thinking of one night

when we'd returned from a singing tour. We were all exhausted and, therefore, a little high-strung. The girls were trying to talk Pat into something or other, and he was beginning to steam. I don't remember what the issue was, but I remember the rising anger in Pat's voice as he brought the discussion to a head.

"I appreciate everything you've said, girls. I've listened but the answer is no. You simply can't do that," he said, having already explained in detail his reasons.

I wasn't in the room, so I don't know what Lindy said, but it sounded sassy to Pat, and he thought he saw a smirk on her face.

"I just saw red," he said later. And he slapped her!

Lindy is probably the most sensitive of all the girls, a regular human Niagara. She promptly dissolved into tears. The other girls started crying too, and I came running in from the bedroom to see what was happening. Pat was red in the face and shouting.

Nothing makes him boil more quickly than disrespect or impudence from the girls. His folks were like that, and he grew up with a healthy respect for their last word and their spankings.

Don't most parents have to grapple with this over and over? You love your kids, you want the best for them, and you really don't want to have arguments. But they happen, time after time, and tempers flare. Things are said that wound deeply, and sometimes violence erupts. Why is it?

We had yet to discover a vital Bible principle that will work wonders in any family. I'll share it with you in just a moment.

I'll say this about Pat. He doesn't get mad often, but when he does, it's a lulu! But the best part is, he calms down right away, and apologizes. That's what happened in the blowup with Lindy. Within moments he was hugging her and reassuring the girls that he was sorry. Because he acted quickly, the Lord healed the breach, and a good night's sleep erased it. That's happened with us many, many times.

I think that's an important lesson in itself. In the early part of our marriage, I found it difficult to say, "I'm sorry." Those are really magic words. I don't agree with the slogan of the movie *Love Story*: "Love means never having to say you're sorry."

That sounds great to young romantics, but it doesn't work. Very soon in any relationship, situations arise that call for apologies. Either that, or those relationships don't last long.

As usual Jesus has the winning formula, in this case right from Sermon on the Mount: "If therefore you are presenting your offering at the altar, and there remember that your brother has something against you, leave your offering there before the altar, and go your way; first be reconciled to your brother, and then come out and present your offering" (Matthew 5:23, 24 NASB).

Imagine that! Jesus recommends that you stop right in the middle of worship if you remember that someone is waiting to hear you say, "I'm sorry."

Through the years with Pat and the girls, I've seen the wonders an apology works in melting barriers and hard feelings. Sometimes I've even apologized when I didn't feel I'd been wrong. And it didn't hurt a bit! I could tell lots of stories about *my* mistakes—over-protectiveness or just bad judgment. I've had to do more than apologize to the girls. But since this is my chapter, I'll tell on Pat one more time. He can get even with me later.

It was one of the most emotional nights of our lives. We were at the Ohio State Fair in Columbus, and we had just finished what we thought might be our last family show. Lindy and Cherry would be getting married in a couple of months. I got terribly choked up on stage, and asked if I could make a personal statement.

"I wouldn't want this occasion to close without urging you—everyone of you—to really turn yourselves and your families over to God. We may never be on a stage again as a family . . .," (at this point I nearly broke down) "and so we may never have another chance to urge you to let Him rule your lives, for your own sakes," I said.

After the show was over, Governor Rhodes, who was in the

audience, and many others told us that they had been moved to tears. In fact, the audience had given us a prolonged standing ovation!

Still, our emotions were running high, and our thoughts were a little muddled as we packed our costumes into the limousines and returned to the hotel. Debby and one of the other girls had gone with Pat and several of our musicians. When they arrived in the lobby, Pat told the girls to go immediately to their rooms. Meanwhile, he and I were detained talking with some friends. When we finally got away and up to our rooms, all the girls were there and ready for bed—except Debby.

"She was hungry," one of her sisters said, "and went to the vending machines to find something to eat."

We've never liked our girls wandering through hotel halls late at night, but we understood Debby's sweet tooth and figured she'd be right back. It was a slight infraction of Pat's instructions, but this was a special night, so he let it go.

But after a while he asked, "How long has she been gone, now?"

"Oh, maybe twenty minutes," the girls answered.

"I think you should see if you can find her, Pat," I said.

So Pat went looking. She was not at the vending machines on our floor. So he went to the next floor. Still no Debby. Finally, he was at the lobby level, and he headed toward the desk to see if any of our friends had seen her. There was Debby talking to a couple of our musicians.

He thought that when Debby saw him approaching down the hall, she would say to the musicians, "Here comes Daddy. I've been gone quite a while, so I'll see you later."

But not Debby. Instead, she just smiled as Pat got close to her and kept on talking.

Pat interrupted, "What are you doing?"

Quite nonchalantly, Debby answered, "Oh, I just came downstairs to get some candy."

That was a little much for Pat, and he said, "You've been

gone a long time, and I had told you to go straight to your room. Let's go." There was an ominous tone in his voice.

On the way to the room Debby complained, "I wasn't doing anything wrong. I was just going to get some candy and I ran into our guys in the lobby. They wanted to talk for a few minutes; what's wrong with that? After all, I'm nearly eighteen years old."

Back in the room Pat explained there was nothing wrong with talking to our musicians. They were fine guys, and we respected them. He was angry because she had been told to go to the room with the other girls and hadn't done it. He had allowed her more than enough time, but when he had to come looking for her, she had acted as if *he* was the one out of line.

Debby answered back just once too many times, and Pat passed his boiling point. He grabbed Debby, threw her over his knees, and began to spank her soundly. Shocked, the girls started to cry, and I was about to intercede when the phone rang. It was one of the musicians.

"I'd like to come up and talk with you," he told Pat. "I'm afraid I got Debby in trouble, and I'd like to apologize."

"No," Pat answered. "That's not necessary. You haven't done anything wrong; we'll talk about it tomorrow."

But the musician was insistent. "Really, I feel I contributed to the situation, and I'd like to talk to you about it."

"Look," Pat said in exasperation, "it's not your fault. This is between Debby and me. We'll talk tomorrow." And he hung up.

Then, suddenly, Pat seemed to realize what he had done. He felt embarrassed at his impatience in front of the musicians.

And all the rest of us were sobbing. I was especially distressed, because Pat and Debby had had a difficult time in the last several years. Just when it appeared they had it all worked out—this happened. I knew Debby had really met the Lord and was filled with His Spirit, but I was afraid this might trigger some new streak of rebellion.

Pat and I went to our room and sat down on the bed. He was

near tears himself, feeling miserable. We sat and prayed silently for a while, and then got up and went back to the girls' rooms.

"I'm sorry, girls," he said. "And I'm especially sorry for your sake, Debby. I'm afraid your Daddy was out of line. I shouldn't have lost my temper that way; I'm not saying that what you did was right, but I may have been more wrong than you. I don't think what you did or said deserved the spanking. And I'm apologizing to all of you, especially to you, Deb."

The girls managed to mumble something in response.

It wasn't a typical "Partridge Family" ending. I don't remember any kisses being exchanged that night; we just all said "goodnight" and went to bed.

But the next day was beautiful! As we flew home, Debby went out of her way to sit next to her Daddy and laughingly referred to the black and blue marks on her bottom. We all had a good laugh. I think Pat was especially grateful that we did—because he could blame the tears in his eyes on the laughter.

Soon after that, we discovered the principle, and since then we've never had such a blowout on the road, or anywhere else. Paul outlines it in II Timothy 2:23-26 (NASB): "But refuse foolish and ignorant speculations, knowing that they produce quarrels. And the Lord's bond-servant must not be quarrelsome, but be kind to all, able to teach, patient when wronged, with gentleness correcting those who are in opposition; if perhaps God may grant them repentance leading to the knowledge of the truth, and they may come to their senses and escape from the snare of the devil, having been held captive by him to do his will!"

Do you see it? Somehow, we think that these passages only apply to folks "out in the world," or to people at church or in the twilight zone or somewhere. But these principles apply *at home!* And kids won't do it unless their parents set the example.

Believe me, I'm aware of how difficult it is to apply this

principle. It's against my own nature, and without the help of the Holy Spirit, nobody could manage it all the time. As Paul points out, you're not in that family squabble alone—*a supernatural enemy named Satan is right in the midst of it, trying to turn family members against each other!*

How many times have you heard of someone saying, "I don't know why I did that! I can't believe that I hit her that way"?

Or, "I didn't mean to hurt him—I love him! Something came over me!"

"I don't know why I did that. I just lost control, I guess."

Please read that Scripture over again. Ask the Holy Spirit to burn it indelibly into your consciousness, and to remind you of it often. I think I'd word the principle this way: *Strife is the devil's turf. Stay off!*

Throughout the Bible Satan is identified as the source of division, strife, hate and mistrust; he's called the "accuser of the brethren." And Jesus says that in the last days a man's enemies will be those of his own house. But as Christians we have the authority to bind Satan's work in our homes. Pat sensed that we should do this in the situation with Debby. And I feel it helped to clear up the problem.

Are you getting the picture? The family circle, the home, should be the place where we learn to get along with each other. It's not easy; in fact, if you can do it at home, you can do it anywhere!

At home or on the road, we've discovered through painful experience that Paul's "antistrife" principle will avoid blowouts, and the magic words, "I'm sorry," will patch them when they do occur.

It's a good thing the Lord was revealing these principles to us, because we were about to need all the love and compassion and faith we could muster.

13

Skin and Bones—
and Heart

PAT

"Pat, our child is dying right before our eyes!"

I looked at Shirley, not wanting to admit that she might be right. She was struggling to control her emotions, but her eyes were filled with tears, and her hands were shaking.

Cherry, the perky and creative dispenser of joy, our five-foot, seven-inch beauty had dropped to just over ninety pounds! It had sneaked up on us and then hit us like a ton of bricks. Cherry had been long and slim ever since she was seventeen or so. We'd gotten used to that, and though I had often kidded her and urged her to gain some weight, Shirley and I had decided that Cherry's bones were small. Perhaps she was meant to be a willowy model type.

But tonight when she came into our bedroom in her shorty nightgown and lay curled up on our bed between Shirley and me, we were stunned! She had just come in to say good night and visit a few minutes. Her arms and legs seemed like matchsticks, or pipecleaners, and her hip bones protruded almost grotesquely at the base of her spine, which stood out in awful relief in her childlike back. Except for her face, she looked emaciated, wasted—like a concentration camp victim. What in earth had happened?

We had a brief prayer, and Cherry was off to bed. For most of that night, and for countless long and agonizing hours afterward, Shirley and I tried to piece together the possible causes for this alarming situation. We had many talks with Cherry, with her sisters, and prayed a lot. Gradually, the picture developed.

After Cherry broke up with her Mormon boyfriend, she tried to settle back into a normal life pattern. She enrolled at UCLA, and immersed herself in class work. She was studying psychology, tap dancing, anthropology, music, voice, English, and eventually Hebrew. The work load was terrific, but Cherry seemed content to have every waking moment filled with something. We felt it was probably therapeutic.

In addition to the school work, she was writing songs, learning guitar, and, of course, playing a vital role in our family shows. These were taking us to hotels and fairs and concert halls all over the country!

She was greatly concerned about her classmates and friends, often bringing them home with her, where together we could pray for them and share our life in Jesus. She was starting to date a little, and we had no real reason to think anything was wrong.

Shirley was the first to pick up on one thing though. "She's so thin," Shirley said several times, "she's almost skin and bones, yet she's always talking about taking off weight."

I'd noticed that too, but with a wife and four daughters in the same house—diets and calorie charts and teardrops on the bathroom scale are just a part of our daily lives! Cherry had always been meticulous about her appearance, and now she seemed to be on a real health kick. I thought that was great, because I myself am a physical fitness nut, constantly jogging, working out at the gym, and playing tennis or basketball.

And now Cherry was jogging too. Sometimes she ran with me, which made me happy—and other times she ran alone, as much as five miles at a time! I thought that was great, and maybe her skinniness was just a result of a lot of exercise.

But then we began to notice that she was eating huge amounts of food. And it wasn't always healthy stuff. More and more often she was eating large quantities of junk foods, half a cake or a pound or two of cookies! We began to find empty half-gallon ice cream boxes in the wastebasket in her room. It was strange, because she was seemingly so conscious of her health and nutrition, and at the same time gorging on "garbage."

Several times we learned that she had eaten so much that she vomited. As Shirley and I got more concerned and more watchful, we learned that Cherry would sometimes gorge on a lot of ice cream and cake and other stuff, and then deliberately lose the whole mess. Now we knew how she could eat all that food and still be skinny.

Even worse, we saw that she was becoming irritable, and dissatisfied with herself. Clearly, there was a lot of guilt attached to this process. Cherry's too smart not to realize it's wrong to gorge on junk, and then deliberately lose it. So she would go out and exercise more and more—sometimes four or five hours a day!

She fluctuated from extreme to extreme, and nothing Shirley or I said seemed to matter much. After all, Cherry was almost grown now, in college and old enough to be making most of her decisions by herself. As parents, we were trying to "order" less and suggest more. It wasn't working. What were we to do?

If it were just a health problem, I would have been more confident. We'd had lots of bouts with sickness and physical problems, but after our new commitments to the Lord and our constant discovery of the power of the Word and the working of the Holy Spirit, we felt we had those things licked!

In fact, just a year or so before, I'd written the book, *A Miracle a Day Keeps the Devil Away,* and one of my chapters was "The Miracle of Health." I had quoted Jesus' promise in

Mark 16:17, 18 and Peter's bold declaration in I Peter 2:24. Then I gave a dramatic example of how these Scriptures have worked in my life.

For fifteen years I had suffered a couple of vicious virus attacks every year like clock work. I could count on them; they never let me down. They always hit me in the spring and fall, strangling my throat, filling my sinuses, and taking my voice away.

And the allergies! I'd never had allergies when I was growing up in Tennessee. But after I moved to California, I had increasingly severe attacks each spring and fall. First came the sneezing. Then my eyes got puffy and red. My nose ran—and more often than not, the allergy set the stage for the virus attack. It was a vicious circle.

But after I was filled with the Spirit, I read those Scriptures I mentioned and others, and I decided I didn't have to go through this any longer. It seemed that the olive trees, so prevalent in California, caused my allergy attacks. So I walked out onto the patio and looked up at our biggest olive tree and said, "Okay, tree—it's you or me! And, Satan, if you're mixed up in this thing somehow, I'm rebuking you in the name of Jesus Christ, according to Mark 16:18. I can't help taking in this pollen, which may be a poison in my system, but Jesus says it doesn't have to harm me—and I'm claiming His promise."

I sat down in a chair on the patio and started reading a book. My nose ran, my eyes still swelled up, but I refused to sneeze. I jammed my finger against my upper lip, squeezed my nose and quoted Scripture. And I took big gulping breaths, daring the pollen particles to have any effect on me. My chest tickled, but I would just take deeper breaths.

A victory occurred that day, and *my allergy attacks have vanished completely!* And while I was writing the chapter in *A Miracle a Day,* I hadn't had a virus attack in five years!

But right after I typed the last few words of that chapter, I came down with a raging flu! I resisted it with everything in me; I claimed all the promises; I read the Scriptures and refused to take medicine, but finally had to give in and go to bed. I was mortified. After a couple of days, as I was starting to feel better but still weak, I got down on my knees before the Lord.

"Why did this happen, Father?" I asked. "What door did I leave open so that Satan could gain the advantage over me? Please show me what I did wrong."

While I was praying, two disconnected words floated into my consciousness: *body* and *blood*.

"What does that mean, Lord?"

In that instant I remembered Paul's teaching about the Lord's supper in I Corinthians 11. The Christians in Corinth were losing sight of the meaning and power of that memorial, and Paul gave them a powerful teaching.

He wound it up with this: "That is why a man should examine himself carefully before eating the bread and drinking from the cup. For if he eats the bread and drinks from the cup unworthily, not thinking about the body of Christ and what it means, he is eating and drinking God's judgment upon himself; for he is trifling with the death of Christ. *That is why many of you are weak and sick,* and some have even died. But if you carefully examine yourselves before eating you will not need to be judged and punished. Yet, when we are judged and punished by the Lord, it is so that we will not be condemned with the rest of the world" (TLB).

I knew all that. *But wait—wait a minute,* I asked myself suddenly, *how long has it been since I actually communed with the Lord this way?*

It was all clear now. I realized that I had been on the road for quite a while, and had missed the opportunity to take communion in a regular worship service. And I'd been so busy—doing all kinds of good things, I told myself— that I hadn't taken a few quiet moments to commune with the Lord on my own. It had probably been a couple of months!

"That is why many of you are weak and sick . . . ." Immediately, on wobbly knees I went downstairs, got some unleavened bread, and grape juice and came back to my room and had a wonderful time communing with the Lord and worshipping my slain and risen Savior. I was well overnight! And I haven't been sick since.

I used to think that the Lord's Supper is an experience confined to a church building. But Jesus doesn't say that. He simply says to do it in remembrance of Him. It's not just a ritual; it's not just a memorial service. It's a reminder of *who He is and what He's done,* and that in Him we can be victorious over sin and sickness and every device of the devil. That's why Paul says, "For every time you eat this bread and drink this cup you are retelling the message of the Lord's death, that He has died for you. Do this until He comes again."

We had discovered long since the value of sharing the Lord's Supper as a family. And we'd done it many times, both on the road and at home. And many of our health problems vanished, as well as spiritual ones too.

But Cherry's problem was deeper than anything we'd run up against. We were facing a physical, emotional and spiritual problem, rolled up into one. We tried everything—communion, conferences with Pastor Jack Hayford, consultation with medical authorities. Nothing seemed to help.

Then one day I read an article in *Newsweek* magazine about a sickness striking girls who were usually in middle- or upper-class families. It's called *anorexia nervosa,* and it seems to affect only girls, with rare exceptions. My eyes zoomed in on the article, because it described Cherry perfectly.

I read that there was a classic pattern to this illness: the girls usually had parents who were high achievers, who set up high standards for their children. Seemingly, the girls were well-adjusted and happy, but would alternately gorge and starve themselves. The doctors determined that these actions constituted rebellion against impossibly high expectations, and at the same time were a rigid attempt to totally control their own bodies.

When Cherry read the article, her eyes widened. "That's me!" she said.

And soon after that, we just "happened" to run across other articles in newspapers and magazines on the same malady. We gathered that some of the girls just grew out of the syndrome, but also that there's a 15 percent to 20 percent mortality rate!

This really rattled us, and we got on our knees often and long. We fasted too, although we wondered if that was the right approach for Cherry; but she felt that she wanted to really turn herself over to the Lord. Fasting is certainly the way to do that. In a curious way it seemed to help Cherry to know she wasn't alone in this problem, and pretty soon some of her old gaiety reappeared. She made an obvious attempt to balance her diet.

The Lord had spoken through Oral Roberts in a word of prophecy in our home once, and told Cherry that her special gift was joy. And sure enough, she's always had a unique ability to inspire joy and happiness and fun in others. She has a special ability to do and say just the right thing.

We asked the Holy Spirit to fill her up with overflowing joy. About that time Shirley ran across a verse in Proverbs that says that a merry heart does good like medicine, but a broken spirit drys the bones. That Solomon—once again he had given us the diagnosis and the remedy!

And Jack Hayford gave us a booster shot from Isaiah 58. In that chapter the Lord makes it plain that He's not so interested in our doing penance, but what He wants are deeds that meet the needs of other people!

"Feed the hungry! Help those in trouble! Then your light will shine out from the darkness, and the darkness around you shall be as bright as day. And the Lord will guide you continually, and satisfy you with all good things, and keep you healthy too; and you will be like a well-watered garden, like an ever-flowing spring" (TLB).

There was progress, but still not complete victory. Though her weight increased steadily, from time to time Cherry would fall back into the old patterns, with an accompanying sense of guilt and frustration. It was a real spiritual and emotional tug-of-war. Shirley and I, realizing that we might have unwittingly contributed to this whole mess by expecting too much of our first-born, were at our wits' end.

And then came Dan O'Neill!

One early evening Virginia Otis called to say that her husband, George, had met a young man in Israel who had greatly impressed him. The young man, Dan O'Neill, had spent thirteen months on two kibbutzim, working and praying for Israel. He had returned to speak at a youth conference and was going back to Israel, probably for good. But Virginia felt that Cherry would like to meet him, that they would enjoy talking about Israel and speaking Hebrew together.

Actually, neither Cherry nor Dan was interested in meeting the other. The meeting only took place because they each wanted to please Virginia and didn't know how to say no. Dan, a Spirit-filled Youth with a Mission leader, had decided he would be a bachelor the rest of his life, so that he could serve the Lord like Paul. Meeting girls, any girls, would be a waste of time. And Cherry, still somewhat wounded from her involvement with the Mormon boy, wanted to concentrate on Hebrew and song-writing—not boys. Not even handsome, intelligent, athletic boys like this one.

But thanks to Virginia, they did meet, and they *did* enjoy speaking Hebrew together! In fact, they enjoyed it so much that they decided to get together again, this time with no urging from anybody! It was purely platonic, no pressure, just laughs and Hebrew chatter and lots of talk about Israel and the Lord. After all, Dan was going back to Israel, so this was just a temporary friendship, two ships passing in the night.

Cherry was impressed with Dan's deep spirituality, and she confided in him about her problem with anorexia. She asked Dan to pray with her about it. He took her hands in his, and earnestly asked the Lord to put an end to this hassle, and he firmly forbade Satan to afflict her with it any more. After their prayer, he gave Cherry some solid Youth with a Mission-type advice about personal habits and discipline, and urged her to "hang in there with the Lord and believe that He's done what we've asked." Cherry was different after that.

She told Shirley, "You know, Mamma, when Dan prayed for me, something happened. I know it did; he's really special."

And from the tone in her voice and the look in her eyes, Shirley decided that something really had happened—and not just concerning the anorexia nervosa.

14

The Win-a-Boone-
for-Life Game

PAT

If you watch television at all, you could get the idea that everything involving the American family is either a situation comedy, a soap opera or a game show. Since this chapter intimately involves an American family, I think I'll take the third format.

THE CONTESTANTS

Pat and Shirley Boone: parents

Cherry Boone: intelligent, "foxy" and creative daughter.

Lindy Boone: darkly beautiful, meant to be a wife and mother.

Debby Boone: petite, blonde-knockout, talented singer.

Laury Boone: could've been an Olympic gymnast—lovely, athletic extrovert.

Assorted young men: each trying to walk off with a Boone girl of his own, but sometimes making up his own rules.

I guess we could have called this "The Mating Game." As parents of four reasonably attractive and desirable daughters,

Shirley and I saw it coming a long way off. So we tried to get ready for the onslaught.

Several years ago at an important function in Washington, D.C., our family met Dr. Henry Kissinger, then Secretary of State. He wasn't married yet, and some of the magazines were portraying him as the playboy of the Western world. After I introduced the courtly Mr. Kissinger to our long line of females, he turned to me and in that resonant voice commented, "You haff lovely daughters."

"Thank you, Mr. Secretary," I replied. "Coming from you, that's quite a compliment. You may not have realized it, but we're both connoisseurs of beautiful women."

He chuckled. And then I added, "The only difference is—I grow my own!"

And we all had a good laugh. But there was a serious side to it too. As specialists in girl-production, Shirley and I have realized that we'd better have quality control and a good working system, or we'd be in for lots of trouble.

RULES OF THE GAME
Way back when the girls were in elementary school and just starting to think ahead about boys, dating and romantic things, Shirley and I began to tell them how it would be. We figured that if we laid out some simple rules early enough and stuck to them, we might make it through those teenage years alive.

After prayerful thought, we decided there would be no single dating until each girl was sixteen. For a couple of years before that they could date in groups with a proper chaperone, if we knew where they were and what was going on—(as much as any parent ever does, really). Any single dating before sixteen would naturally imply that the boy was at least a year or two older than our daughter, or he wouldn't be licensed to drive. Shirley would be in charge of makeup and dress supervision, and Daddy would butt in only if Mama hit a snag, some lack of cooperation.

136

Then we insisted on knowing the boy. I know a lot of families let their daughters go out with guys the parents have never met, but we made it clear that if any of our girls wanted to date a guy, she should invite him to the house. The girls could ask their boyfriends over for dinner, to watch TV, play pool, maybe challenge old Dad to a basketball or volleyball competition, and just fit in, in general. He'd be invited to go to church with us, and maybe come to our local performance after we started singing together. We wanted to "test the water," see how he fit into our family style, and give him the opportunity to see if he liked our way of doing things.

I had the sneaky feeling that if a guy enjoyed being around our family, he was a fairly safe dating bet. If he wanted nothing to do with our family, just wanted to drop by to take one of the girls away and drop her off at the end of an evening without getting involved with the rest of us, he was likely to find Poppa Pat arm-wrestling him at the front door!

By the time the girls got old enough to start dating seriously, we had added another proviso: with rare exceptions the young man should be a Christian. That automatically made for common ground, a probable understanding of our protective rules and moral guidelines, and would save a lot of heartache in case the romance became serious. There were many more details, but I've given the basic rules of the game.

DO NOT PASS GO; DO NOT COLLECT BOONE GIRL; GO DIRECTLY TO PENALTY BOX.

Here's an example of the way we employed the rules, and how one guy lost. Our family had been doing one of the Japanese Maxwell House commercials, and in the course of several days' filming, one of the fellows on the crew was strongly attracted to one of our daughters (I won't say which one because of potential embarrassment. I will say that she was seventeen at the time).

He wouldn't tell her how old he was, but he was the kind of guy that most young girls flip over. Tall and lean, lots of black, curly hair, flashing smile and debonair "I've been around and know the score" kind of attitude. He had a good sense of humor and charming ways. All the girls thought he was cute, but he zeroed in on one in particular.

After our filming was done, he called her several times at home and asked her for a date. He was absolutely amazed when she said, "I'll have to ask my parents."

When she approached us about this, Shirley and I tried to keep an open mind.

"Honey, I'm afraid he's too old for you, and we don't know much about him. Still, we don't want to close the door completely. Why don't you bring him to one of our shows at Magic Mountain? It won't be an official date, but we'll have a chance to get to know him better, and he can look us over as a family. We'll see where it goes from there.

"You can invite him to go to church with us Sunday and have lunch with us afterwards. If he's comfortable in our family activities—and once we know how old he is—then we'll make a decision about actual dating. Okay?"

I guess it was embarrassing for her to relay this to the fellow, but she did it, and he came along with us to Magic Mountain. He didn't accept the invitation to go to church with us, and soon was out of town on some location filming. He called our daughter pretty frequently, though, and courted her long distance. Shirley and I began to get more and more uneasy about the situation, especially since he never would tell her his age. I could see she was flattered by his attention, and I sensed trouble brewing. So I insisted that there be no dating until we knew his age.

It turned out he was 31! That settled it, of course. I gave our daughter the choice of breaking the news to him herself or letting me do it. She asked if she could have an hour with him to explain our rules and priorities and let him down easy. Besides she knew now that he wasn't a Christian and hoped that their long-range association would result in his coming to know the Lord. She wanted to handle the matter with tact and kindness.

"Can we go over to the park, or can we just take a drive in his car?" she asked.

"No, Honey, the age factor rules that out. He can come here, and you can have an hour or two together, but I suggest you sit out in the side yard where you can have privacy. You'll be out of hearing but not necessarily out of sight," I answered.

She understood without my having to explain. So he came over, and they sat out on a picnic blanket in the side yard. I just "happened" to pass the window several times and noticed that they were having a serious, sometimes animated discussion. I got the impression he was doing a real "hard sell" job.

After they'd had a reasonable amount of time, I ambled out and asked if I could join them.

They both said, "Fine, sit down," and made room for me on the blanket.

He said, "You have quite a daughter here. She's a very special young lady. She's been explaining to me the way your family does things, and it all makes sense to me except your worry about this age difference. I don't think numbers mean anything."

"They may not mean anything to you," I answered, "but this girl is only seventeen. She hasn't dated much and hasn't had the kind of experience that you've had. As her father I just don't think it's wise for her to date someone fourteen years older than she is. We like you, we really do, and you're welcome to go to church with us and be involved in some of our family activities. But as far as single dating is concerned, I'm afraid you'll have to wait until she's older—at least two or three years."

He was exasperated and said so. "I agree with the way you and Shirley are bringing up your girls, except for this age thing. I'll tell you frankly, I've already been through the sex and the drugs, and I'm more settled now. I think I'd be better for your daughter than some young kid who's still experimenting with those things!" he said.

I glanced at her and told him, "We're not planning for our

girls to date boys who are experimenting; and I don't think they want to anyway."

I realize it was difficult for him to see my viewpoint, because he'd been brought up without any spiritual training. I told him the story of Jacob in the Bible, his experience with Rachel and Leah, and how their father had forced Jacob to work fourteen years just to marry Rachel.

"I'd never do that," he said.

"Well, few people would," I said. "But because Jacob did, and because he met his father-in-law's conditions, he became the ancestor of the twelve tribes of Israel and of David and the Messiah. So there are definite advantages to waiting and doing things God's way."

I left them alone for a little while longer, and they had a sorrowful good-by. He wasn't willing to wait, and our daughter realized that this was not a match made in heaven. But she had grown to care about him and promised she would pray for him. Soon enough she realized that she had been courting disaster and became much more cautious in forming emotional attachments. And Shirley and I spent some time on our knees thanking the Lord!

A GROUND-RULES DOUBLE

Lindy has always seemed the least complicated of our gals. Shirley remembers a time when the girls were smaller, and she'd been talking seriously with Debby and Cherry about their problems. Suddenly, Lindy clouded up with tears.

"Lindy," Shirley asked her, "what's the matter?"

"You're always helping the other girls with their problems," Lindy cried, "and I don't have any problems!"

And praise the Lord, she didn't! Lindy has always taken the straight-ahead approach, been the most trusting and obedient, and always seemed so balanced and able to handle any assignment with hard work and concentration.

Well—she did have one small flaw. She could be absent-minded. Like the day at Pepperdine University during her freshman year when she had driven her Pontiac LeMans out to the beautiful Malibu campus. Some mornings she'd be so busy selecting a Bible teaching cassette for the car stereo that she would leave her school books and assignments at home, but this morning she seemed to have it all together.

Until she saw a certain boy heading her way across the campus. She didn't want to talk to him, so she quickly pulled into the first parking space, got out, locked the door and started away.

"Hey!—Hey, Lindy! Wait a minute!" the boy shouted, running toward her.

Lindy turned and discovered that she had left the keys in the car with the motor still running! By the time they jimmied the car door open, she was out of gas.

So knowing and loving Lindy as I did, I really wasn't ready when she looked at me across the dining room table, barely eighteen years old, and said, "Daddy, Doug and I want to get married."

Married! Married? My eighteen-year-old college freshman, still so sweet and innocent and vulnerable, not even my oldest daughter? Married? I couldn't believe my ears. I couldn't take it in. Surely this was some kind of practical joke on poor ol' Daddy.

Actually, Cherry and Shirley had met Doug first at Hal Lindsey's Bible class in Westwood. Shirley's eye kept turning toward this tall, clean, athletic-looking young fellow across the room. He seemed to look her way every now and then, and Shirley wondered if she'd met him before, possibly at church or somewhere. The thought crossed her mind that he might be the right kind of young man for Cherry to know. After all, he must be a Christian to be in a Bible class on Wednesday night!

After the class they had talked, discovered they had a mutual friend and that Doug was there in the Bible class because he was really interested in moving on with the Lord. He had committed his life to Jesus just a couple of years earlier and now was curious about the baptism in the Holy Spirit. He had a couple of Spirit-filled roommates at Pepperdine University, where he was a senior and a star baseball pitcher!

"I have a book that I think will be helpful to you," Shirley told him. "I'll have Cherry's sister, Lindy, bring it to you at school tomorrow; she's at Pepperdine too."

And you can take it from there. Lindy did take Doug the book; he took a few good looks at Lindy and their story began. Before long, Doug was seeing a lot of Lindy on campus, then dropping by after school for casual visits at the house, sometimes staying for dinner. We liked him tremendously. Though he was three years older than Lindy, he wasn't pushing or hurrying or putting pressure on Lindy. He seemed to genuinely like her and us. Most of our discussions centered on his growth in the Lord and their mutual school involvements. Their friendship seemed fine to me.

Friendship? One day late that fall, Lindy drove home from school, and Shirley noticed her face seemed flushed.

"Lindy, is something bothering you?" Shirley asked her.

They took a walk around the block and talked about it. "Mama, I don't know what to think. Doug and I usually talk after class at school, and today we prayed. It was Doug's idea, and we really prayed that God would show us what our relationship is supposed to be. I think I love him, Mama; he thinks he loves me too. But we realize we haven't known each other very long, and we just want to know God's will for us."

So gentle, so earnest, so right. Although the idea was laden with heavy possibilities and so sudden, the sweetness of Doug and Lindy's yieldedness to the Lord softened the blow and gave Shirley confidence about it.

"Look, Lindy," she said, "it's going to be okay. If both of you tell God that you want to love and serve Him above all else, He'll show you what your relationship to each other should be. Doug's older than you are, but he's a fine Christian. I believe God will watch over you. Just don't get in a hurry."

When Shirley told me about this, I almost laughed, in spite of the clutching feeling around my heart. I was grateful that they were approaching things so seriously and spiritually, but surely this was just a passing thing. I kept thinking that when Doug was over almost every afternoon, when we all sat together at church, and when he arranged for us to meet his folks.

Then one evening Shirley turned to me out of the blue and said, "I believe the Lord just spoke to me that Doug is the one for Lindy."

"Well," I answered, "we'll wait a year or two and see."

But it was just after New Year's when Doug and Lindy asked if they could talk to Shirley and me in the dining room. Why did I feel like a condemned man heading toward that little room at the end of the hall? That's when they dropped the bomb on us. Brave but flushed, holding hands fiercely under the table, (much as Shirley and I when I asked Red Foley if I could marry *his* daughter) they quietly let us know that they felt the Lord had put them together and wanted our permission to become engaged.

How I managed to sit there and smile and talk so calmly, I'll never know. Maybe it was because Shirley seemed to think it was a great idea! In a way history was repeating itself, because Shirley says she "knew" that we were going to get married, while we were still seniors in high school. I guess we did both really love each other from the time we were seventeen or so, though we waited a couple of years to get married. I struggled for wisdom.

"God may very well have picked you two out for each other," I said, "but let's not rush anything. Feeling the way you do about each other, this could be a dangerous time. Doug, Lindy is going to have to keep our normal dating rules. In fact, I'm going to be even more cautious now, *because* you seem so serious. If you feel this deeply about Lindy, you'll have to submit to the restrictions. We can't release her to the kind of freedom you're used to. This could be a tough time for you. Do you understand what I'm saying?"

"That's all right with me," Doug answered calmly. "I

understand your position as father, and I really believe in the way you're raising Lindy. I've already had my flings, and the Lord has shown me a better way. We just want what He wants, and I know it would take some time for me to prove to you and Shirley that I can be a good husband for Lindy. Whatever you say goes. If you don't want us to date at all, we'll accept that, but if you do, you can set any kind of restrictions on our dating that you want, and we'll abide by them. Right, Lindy?"

And Lindy nodded, beaming like a Cheshire cat.

Well, it would take another book to describe their courtship which went on *for two years!* Yes, here was a strapping, healthy twenty-two-year-old university senior, who had to get his date back home by 11:00 p.m.! I can just imagine the razzing he got from his friends. But Doug and Lindy hung in there, even when occasionally I had to say no to some school function that would keep them out after midnight, our absolute outside deadline.

"Lindy is your daughter, under your authority," Doug said. "I realize that if I want her to submit to me some day, my assignment is to submit to you."

My defenses gradually melted. Doug loved being around our house, involved in our family activity, worshipping with us, and kidding with our other daughters, who came to love him too. So after Doug and Lindy had been dating almost a year under these controlled conditions, we allowed them to pick a wedding date. Doug bought Lindy a beautiful engagement ring. It was a big night—and we all felt great about it—even me!

Then Dan and Cherry hit me with bomb number 2! After Dan and Cherry had met, used all their Hebrew vocabulary, after Dan had prayed for Cherry and seen a remarkable improvement in her, he indefinitely postponed his return to Israel. He went to work for George Otis at Bible Voice, and settled into book and TV production with George's company.

He and Cherry spent a lot of time together, and Dan fit into our family situation just as Doug had. In fact, he and Doug wound up sharing an apartment together, along with two other Christian young men. Four guys in a cluttered apartment, sharing laughs and dirty laundry and fellowship in the Lord. Months went by, and Cherry and Dan grew close and deeply committed to each other.

In the spring of Lindy's wedding year, George Otis asked Dan and Cherry to accompany him to Israel to work with the tour group he was taking. Dan was to be coordinator, tour guide and translator. Cherry was to be the chief musician, teaching Israeli songs to the tour members, both in English and in Hebrew. Shortly before departure day, Cherry asked Shirley and me if we'd come out in the backyard, sit on a blanket and talk with her and Dan.

Again that old clutching feeling around my heart, the long trudge up the dark corridor toward the dimly lit room. . . . Surprise! This time it was easier! It was a bright, sunny day, and again Shirley seemed radiant. We knew that Dan had been wonderful for Cherry and she seemed to bring out good things in him too. And after all, she was twenty years old, and he twenty-six, settled in his relationship with Jesus, and as mature, dependable and dedicated as a father-in-law could wish.

So we agreed that they could become engaged after they returned from Israel. We laid out some fairly strict gound rules, which Dan readily agreed to. His attitude toward me was the same as Doug's, recognizing my position as a concerned father and Cherry's spiritual covering. So now we were going to give up two of our daughters, possibly in the same year.

How can I describe the joy of a situation like this, where two young men voluntarily submit themselves to an awkward, fumbling father because of their allegiance to the Lord and because they know it's right? What could have been a traumatic time for Shirley and me became a period of happiness, confidence and joyful expectancy. Whenever I had to say no to plans that either of the couples made, they accepted it with good grace and made alternate plans with scarcely a ripple in the water. The only reason any of this was possible was that *we were all submitted to the Lord and determined to do it His way.*

But then almost predictably—trouble came to Paradise.

After much prayer and seeking the Lord, Cherry and Dan settled on October 4th as their wedding date. Almost two months *before* Doug and Lindy!

15
D-Day Double

PAT

All her life Lindy had been number 2. She was second in age, second in grades, the second to date and wear makeup and plunge into the dating whirl. She always felt overshadowed by her creative, outgoing, intelligent older sister.

She loved Cherry and was proud of her, and she had her own friends and interests. There was no apparent competition between them; Lindy just believed that Cherry was out in front, and always would be.

But a curious and wonderful thing happened to her during her engagement to Doug. A warm glow, a confidence, a joyous sort of self-assurance rose to the surface, as Lindy realized that for once in her life she was going to be number 1. She was going to be the first of the Boone girls to be married, and she and Doug and Shirley were happily involved in plans for a big church wedding. The date was set for November 29th, two days after Thanksgiving.

Then Dan announced to Cherry that the Lord had shown him *they were to be married October 4th!* There were no big shockwaves around our house, and none of us were taking this as final. But when Lindy heard it, she wept silently for a long time. We all understood and sympathized. Cherry and Dan both were willing to take a later date, even after the first of the year, but there were some evidences, at least to Dan and Cherry, that the Lord had spoken about October 4th for them.

As we mulled it over we were reminded that Dan and Cherry had a strong desire to minister to the Jews. All of Jewish custom and tradition indicates that the oldest daughter in the family should marry first. This goes all the way back to Rachel and Leah, the daughters of Laban, and their husband Jacob. None of us felt that had to be a deciding factor, but it was a contributing influence.

Actually, everybody seemed willing for either couple to marry first—Shirley and I, Dan and Cherry, and Doug—everybody but Lindy. And even she told us quite earnestly that she would accept whatever happened as God's will; but she couldn't hide her feelings. It would be tough for her to be number 2 again.

All of her friends, and a good many of ours, were urging us to let Lindy and Doug be married first. But our minister, Jack Hayford, came up with an interesting observation.

"It seems to me that the Lord is trying to do something for Lindy. It really doesn't matter who's married first, especially since there's less than two months between the wedding dates, and everybody seems thoroughly agreeable to step aside for the other, and only Lindy is having some real torment about it. No matter which wedding comes first, both daughters and their husbands are going to be so absorbed with their marriages and new relationships that none of this will really matter—unless there might be lingering hard feelings between Lindy and Cherry. It may be that the Lord wants to release Lindy forever from the feeling that she is number 2.

"Remember, Lindy and Doug asked me to marry them on November 29th. If they had asked me for early October before I left for Israel, I was available. But they didn't ask and now that option is gone. I don't think any of this has taken the Lord by surprise. He may be working out His purpose in it."

By midsummer it was clear that a showdown was coming. A decision had to be made, and it looked like *I* was going to have to make it! Both the boys were willing to take my verdict as from the Lord, and the girls and Shirley vowed that they were too.

I didn't feel equipped to make that decision, nor did I particularly want to. I wanted what was best for all, and only God knew what that was. So we set a date in July to have dinner together and spend the rest of the evening in prayer, listening for the Lord's instruction.

In preparation for that date, I started restudying what it meant for a man to be a prophet in his own house. Remember the time the Lord spoke through Lindy to me, urging me to exercise the gift of prophecy in our family worship times? Well, I had spoken prophetically to my family a number of times since then, but not for quite a while. And my prophetic utterances were generally short exhortations toward commitment and praise. I knew that Paul in I Corinthians 12 and 14 urges Christians to "desire spiritual gifts, but especially the gift of prophecy." As I studied the various times in the Bible where people exercised this gift, I came up with my own simple definition: *prophecy is speaking the will of God under the anointing of the Holy Spirit.*

In Numbers 11 the Holy Spirit fell on seventy men at one time, and they all began to prophesy. This was evidence that God was sharing Moses' massive burden with them. In Acts 21 Agabus came to Philip's house in Caesarea to prophesy to Paul that if he went to Jerusalem, he would be bound and delivered into the hands of the Gentiles.

That same chapter says that Philip the evangelist, one of the seven original deacons in Jerusalem, had four virgin daughters who were prophetesses! *(I got goose bumps reading that because I had four virginal daughters, each of whom had spoken the will of God under the anointing of the Holy Spirit. I hope to have a long talk with Philip some day and find out what it was like at his house with his four daughters!*

I knew God wants each believing man to be priest and prophet in his own home. Also I knew of three aspects of a prophet's role. A prophet should *witness* to his faith; he should *proclaim* the word of truth according to the Scriptures and God's revealed will; and if the Lord prompted him, he might also *predict,* or foretell some aspect of the Lord's plan. This was the pattern I found operating among prophets of God under the old and new covenants.

I really didn't know what the Lord would want to speak through me, but I sensed we were in for a memorable night. When it came Shirley fixed a wonderful dinner, as usual, and afterward we shut off the TV and gathered in the den and began to worship the Lord.

For a while we sang and prayed and praised our mighty King. Periodically, we stopped for quiet discussion, during which each of us expressed submission to the will of God and a desire for whatever would most bless the others. It was really beautiful. Toward midnight there was an air of quiet calm and readiness for whatever the Lord wanted to say. I knew the moment had come.

We joined hands and earnestly came before God again. I opened my mouth and began to speak. It was a real step of faith because I didn't know from word to word what the full message would be. It was almost as if I were listening, though it was my own voice I heard. I don't remember the exact wording, but afterwards we all pieced together this paraphrase:

"Children, the Lord your God loves you more than you can know and is pleased with your willingness to seek His will. Because you seek and because you believe, His will shall be accomplished in and through you.

"Girls, you are like lovely flowers to your God. He has created each of you and made each of you uniquely beautiful in His sight. As with the flowers of the field, or in any garden, each comes to its own growing and blooming time, bearing its blossoms and reaching its full beauty at its own appointed time. Don't you know that it is in the very design of God for this to be so?

"Do you think that one flower gives Him more pleasure because it blooms earlier than another? No, the reverse is true. The Lord is continually pleased *because* His flowers bloom at different times, and each brings forth her flower and her fruit at exactly the time that brings Him the most pleasure.

"Rachel should not worry. In time past with my servant Jacob she felt neglected because she had to wait. And after she was married, she felt herself a failure because she had only two children, while her sister Leah had many. The Lord loved Leah, and the Lord loved Rachel, and He had His way with each of them. Though Rachel had but two children, they were Joseph and Benjamin—a special delight to the Lord and to their father Jacob. Rachel should not worry, but simply be willing to bring forth the pleasure and the promise of the Lord."

The two girls hugged. With a tender smile Cherry said, "Lindy, I promise you'll be first to have a child."

We all laughed nervously, but we were all relieved that a decision had been made—and we believe, made by the Lord.

Later, Lindy said the Lord gave her a special, sweet confirmation of the original message as she read the 20th chapter of Matthew. This is a well-known parable of the landowner who engaged different laborers at different times of the day, but gave them each the same wage! When those that had worked all day complained because they were being paid no more than the last workers, Jesus had the landowner reply: "Is it not lawful for me to do what I wish with what is my own? Yes, the last shall be first, and the first last."

But the Lord's message that night was not just for the girls. He had something for the boys! And again it came through me. "My servant Jacob also had to wait for my blessing and postpone his own plans and ambitions in submission to his father-in-law, Laban. In the eyes of men his long wait was unjust, but through his submission to the Lord and Laban he reaped a great harvest and became the ancestor of the twelve tribes of Israel, King David and the Messiah. Be willing to wait for the Lord's blessing, and it shall surely come."

Shirley said she knew then that it was the Lord speaking and not me!

"I know you would never say anything like that on your own. It's just not like you to assert your will over someone else's in that kind of situation, and especially not Doug's or Dan's. That had to be the Lord speaking through you."

And I'm sure she's right, so I praise the Lord for His faithfulness and His willingness to be involved in our daily lives.

Maybe you'll think that we were making a mountain out of a molehill here, or that we were being superstitious, mystical, or overprotective. But I don't think so. I know we were at a crossroads then, not just in our lives, but in the lives of our children and perhaps generations to come. *We wanted the guidance of God!*

Everything went beautifully after that. Cherry and Dan had a combined Hebrew-Christian ceremony, first at Church on the Way with Jack Hayford officiating, and then the reception at Bel Air Country Club with Rabbi Silverman from Sinai Temple coming over as the sun went down (he couldn't travel until Sabbath was over). He pronounced blessings on the bride and groom both in Hebrew and in English and explained some Jewish marriage customs. It was all more beautiful than I can describe.

Well, on November 29th Doug and Lindy had the most gorgeous, truly Christian wedding we could ever want. Church on the Way was jammed, and the reception at Sportsman's Lodge was fantastic, with food and beverages flowing and live music serenading hundreds of celebrants and well-wishers. After many tearful and joyful hours, Doug and Lindy were off to Hawaii for a classic honeymoon.

In both weddings old crumbly chin Daddy had to try to sing. Through quavery voice and teary eyes, I did my best with "Sunrise Sunset" at Cherry's wedding and "Father of Girls" at Lindy's. My singing was lousy, but the two brides, the grooms and their own marvelous families seemed to enjoy it—and that's all that mattered. Frankly, I don't remember much about it myself.

Obviously, that's not the end of the story. Cherry and Dan and Doug and Lindy are just starting their stories, but for Lindy there is an exciting first chapter.

In March of the following year about five months after their wedding, Doug and Lindy went with our family and George Otis on a tour of Israel. We had 920 pilgrims with us, and we planted trees and gave blood and stomped all over the Holy Land.

A few weeks after we got back, Lindy and Cherry were together and called one afternoon to talk to Shirley. There was mystery and excitement in Lindy's voice.

"Mom," she said, "I'm pregnant."

Cherry's words had been prophetic. She and Dan were together with Lindy and Doug at their apartment, and they all had a big, joyous celebration.

After a happy and trouble-free pregnancy, Ryan Patrick Corbin arrived on November 12th, 1976. And if anybody in this world is happier than Doug and Lindy, it must be Harry and Vera Corbin and Pat and Shirley Boone. A whole new era is beginning for all of us.

And at long last, Lindy was number 1! Isn't the Lord good?

16

Blooming Where
We're Planted

SHIRLEY & PAT

Pat: Many times I get the feeling that my family lives in a fishbowl filled with piranha, those South American cannibal fish.

For twenty years, I've been in the spotlight most of the time and enjoyed it. My personality and temperament seem perfect for the demands constantly made on an entertainer. In addition to that, Shirley and I have written books and been interviewed for magazine articles, in which we have "spilled our guts," shared some of the most intimate happenings in our lives to help others. So we've lived in a fishbowl by choice.

But when we start getting bitten and chewed on from all sides, I often wonder, *Where did we go wrong?*

Shirley: Yes, I guess the hardest thing for me to handle is criticism—especially when it comes from someone I love. And since we're trying to sow the "Gospel seed" in some very rocky soil, criticism from other Christians really hurts.

I know they mean well, and maybe they're right in some ways, but they can't possibly know what our thinking is or how the Lord may be leading us. It's not always obvious.

Pat: Let me give a "for instance." Not too long ago, I appeared on TV with Cher. For most of the hour, Franky Avalon and Dion and I teamed up with Cher to relive some of the musical highlights of the 1950s. It was a good show and got a high rating. But *I* got letters!

"When you stood there beside Cher, all I could see was her navel sticking out," one man wrote. "Are you sure you're a Christian? What was your reason for being on that show in the first place?"

I pondered his letter for a while then wrote, "What were you doing watching it?"

Other people complained about the dancers behind me in my big production number, and still others objected to the overall tone of the show or to the humor. I tried to answer these letters and explain my reasons for accepting the invitation and why I was praising the Lord for the opportunity.

Shirley: The Cher show came up while we were in the middle of re-examining our position as Christians in the entertainment business. Lots of brothers and sisters were writing to us, telling us to get out of show business, saying things like "light should have no part with darkness," and "let not your good be evil spoken of," and things like that.

Those are certainly valid bits of spiritual advice. But it appeared to us that they must be balanced with "you are the salt of the earth," "be ye in the world but not part of it," and Jesus' own answer when He was criticized for associating with sinners, "I came to minister to those that are sick, not to those that are well."

Pat: Even some Christian leaders stated publicly that I was "playing both ends against the middle," that Hollywood entertainers who professed Christ should get out of the entertainment business and quit singing in hotels and nightclubs that serve liquor. It was a "compromise" with the world.

You know, there aren't many restaurants these days that don't serve liquor, or supermarkets that don't sell it. So I did not really consider that argument a valid one.

But the idea that Christians and church leaders might think us hypocritical or shallow or even damaging to the cause of Christ deeply troubled me. I even considered getting out of the entertainment business totally, and perhaps mounting some evangelistic crusade. What we really wanted was the Lord's will for us.

Shirley: And at the same time, your agents were putting the heat on you to play down the "religious bit."

Pat: Boy, did they!

"Can't you go on TV without talking about Jesus?" they would ask. "Can't you just talk about your records or your entertainment activity or *something* besides your religion? People are going to think you're a preacher."

It was a real tussle, with my professional advisors telling me I was too religious and my spiritual advisors telling me I wasn't religious enough! And in the middle of all this clamor, we were trying to hear God's still, small voice.

Shirley: I was concerned about our girls, as usual. I wondered if we were misleading our own daughters by involving them in the entertainment world. But on the other hand, I was learning to look at Pat's life as a whole, not divided into two or three distinct parts. He was, and is, an entertainer, but he's also a committed Christian, a father, an author and other things. All those pieces put together are what the Lord has made him to be.

What was it that writer asked you in Chicago?

Pat: Oh, yes—it was at a press conference before the big Jesus rally there. He was with one of the big newspapers and asked me, "What percentage of your time do you give to Christian activities?"

I thought about it a minute and answered, "One hundred percent!"

The writer looked puzzled because I had been on the "Tonight Show" just a couple of days before.

"You see," I went on, "I'm a 100 percent Christian. This means that everything I do is a Christian activity. I don't know that the Lord is happy with everything I do, but whatever I do, I do it as a Christian. Therefore, it's a Christian activity."

Shirley: That made sense to me when you said it, but then the letters of criticism and warning shook me up again. There was even one from a devoted Christian woman, who sent an audio cassette for us to listen to. In what she believed was a prophetic utterance, she warned us that if we stayed in the entertainment business, the Lord would cease to use us and that one of our girls would suffer!

You can imagine the effect on me, as close as my girls and I have been. We spent a lot of time on our knees about that, asking the Lord for guidance.

Pat: Then He began to give us some definite indications of what He wanted us to do. They were like little flags blowing in the wind, giving us the Holy Spirit's direction.

"The Cher Show" was one of the flags.

I knew, and later explained to all of the letter writers, that this TV show was not a religious program. It was one of the top-rated shows on television just then, and thirty million or more people would be watching. Would Jesus have me pass up an opportunity like that?

So I agreed to do the show. I looked forward to it. The producers asked me to come up with some kind of solo number, and I walked into CBS with about twenty albums with all kinds of "message" songs that I would like to do on that program. Some of them I had already recorded on my Lamb and Lion music albums. Any one of them would have been a tremendous witness.

But the staff turned thumbs down on all of them. For one reason or another, they felt none of these songs would fit the show or do me justice in a solo spot.

Shirley: Didn't they suggest songs themselves?

Pat: Yes, but most of the things they suggested were unacceptable to me. So we were really at an impasse, and time was running out. You and I prayed about it together, as I remember, and told the Lord, "Father, we just can't seem to find the right song. If You'll select one for me, one that suits You and will be acceptable to them, I'll sing it. Otherwise, I guess I'll just have to pick a wholesome secular song, and let it go at that. Maybe just my being on the show will be useful in Your hands somehow; after all, I am filled with Your Spirit, and I know You can touch people without my saying words about Jesus."

I'm paid to be an entertainer, I rationalized, *so I guess I'm going to have to do some straight entertainment and let the witness come through some other way.*

So I went back to CBS, ready to do a rock song I had recorded several years before. My manager liked it. "The Cher Show" people liked it, and I figured that would be it.

Then thirty minutes before the final decision had to be made, an amazing thing happened. The choral director walked in with an album under his arm.

"Have you got your song for the solo spot?" he asked.

"Well, I've got one, and it's good, but I'm not sure that it's the best song for the spot," I responded.

He took the record out of its cover and put it on the player.

"What about this one?" he asked, and then played Donny Hathaway's "Magnificent Sanctuary Band."

I flipped! That was it! It was all about the last days and pictured the Lord marching at the head of redeemed believers. It extended an invitation for people to "join the magnificent sanctuary band" and march on into heaven with Jesus! Best of all, it was written by Dorsey Burnett, a singer/songwriter and fellow member of our Church on the Way!

The CBS people and the Cher production staff all loved it.

"Hey, that's great! That's perfect for the show. What do you think of it, Pat?"

"Man," I said, "it's great!"

And *they* brought it to me! All my praying, all my searching through albums trying to find just the right tune had resulted in a big zero. How much better that the right song had come through them. I had to believe that the Lord guided that situation and was telling me something about my place in the entertainment profession.

Shirley: Still, Pat, it didn't go exactly as you planned, did it?

Pat: No, even though I reworded the last verse and made it into a challenge to the listener, not just to sing and get happy, but to accept Jesus as Lord. And right on "The Cher Show" in front of thirty million people!

But because the main purpose of that show is to entertain, visually as well as audibly, the choreographer got all the girl dancers dressed up in skimpy outfits and had them marching around behind me, banging tambourines. Visually, they were entertaining but spiritually distracting.

Still, I was singing the message loud and clear, and I felt it came through. After all, they've been doing that show for five years or more; how many other times had they given somebody a chance to sing about Jesus?

Shirley: But many dear Christians are disappointed, even wounded, whenever they see you on TV and you don't preach some kind of gospel message.

"Whenever Billy Graham is on TV," some of them say, "he always tells Johnny or Merv or Mike some real gospel facts, and quotes the Bible. Why can't you do this?"

And they're absolutely right; Billy always does. But Billy Graham is an evangelist; you are a singer. They ask Billy Graham on the show *because* he will talk about the Bible and God's answers to their questions. They ask Pat Boone to sing and to entertain. And yet you still manage to talk about the Lord, almost every time you're on.

Pat: Billy Graham and I take a different approach to our witness, but it packs some of the same wallop. I remember the time when we were both on the "Dick Cavett Show."

Dick asked Billy, "Do you still teach those old ideas about no sex outside of marriage?"

Billy replied, "I certainly do. They're not my ideas; they're God's ideas. As long as the Bible is against sex outside of marriage, so am I."

The audience snickered.

Maybe because of that Billy went ahead, "I'll tell you something else, Dick. I was a perfectly normal young man in every way, but I didn't get married until I was 25. When I married, Ruth was the first and only woman I've ever gone to bed with."

And the audience laughed! It was as if Billy had told some hilarious, off-the-wall joke. I was watching in the waiting room, and I saw Billy's face turn red on the monitor.

I was next on the show, and I sang some big rock tune. When I'd finished, I sat down with Dick and Billy. Dick immediately asked if I'd been listening to the conversation. I told him I had.

He asked, "Do you go along with these things Billy Graham is saying?" I knew he was putting me on the spot.

"Yes, I do. But I understand why the audience laughed at what Billy said. I guess by today's standards that *is* pretty funny."

Again the audience snickered, expecting a joke.

"But as the audience laughed," I said, "I thought of one person in America tonight who doesn't find that funny at all—Ruth Graham."

There was a hush in the studio.

"It's sad to me," I continued, "that young people today appreciate commitment in other areas of life—music, sports, politics—and those who succeed are heroes. But in marriage, a fundamental area in anybody's life, commitment before, during, or after, is a joke. And the saddest part is that the people who are laughing at Billy Graham may never experience for themselves the thirty years of happy married life he and Ruth have shared. And they're laughing at *him*."

Well, about that time Dick Cavett decided it was time for a commercial.

Shirley: Of course, there are the other times—like the "Tonight Show" when the Bahai people were on. Pat had already finished his songs and his talk time with Johnny, and then two popular young recording artists came on. It happens that they are involved in the Bahai faith, and they talked about it with Johnny. I knew Pat was straining to get into the conversation and present Jesus, but the opportunity never seemed to come. On those shows it's not polite to "butt in" unless you're asked, or unless there's a definite lull.

Of course, Pat got several letters from zealous young Christians who felt he had "blown it."

Pat: And I felt a little defeated myself. I wrote the people and explained that I take advantage of every opportunity I have, that I pray before every appearance that the Holy Spirit will direct me and speak through me. I was certainly willing that night, but it just seemed that the opportunity didn't open up. I guess nobody bats a thousand percent—and if I goof, I goof. But sometimes the Lord shows me that He accomplished His purpose anyway.

Shirley: And occasionally when we appear at state fairs or in concerts, people who have seen your portrayal of David

Wilkerson in *The Cross and the Switchblade* come, expecting you to preach a sermon or expecting us to do a straight gospel music show. They let us know that they're disappointed because we sang pop songs and did a well-rounded show that included Jesus music, but not exclusively.

"You speak sweet water and bitter out of the same mouth," one young man complained to us.

We never shrug that kind of thing off, because we know his heart is right, and that he can't possibly understand the larger implications of what we're doing. Pat's not there as Dave Wilkerson. He and his family have been paid to attract a large crowd and to entertain them, and then we mix in some Jesus music and whatever witness we can as part of that.

Pat: And what the zealous Christians don't understand is that we "turn off" as many secular people as Christians—and it's usually the critics! City after city, we get blasted in the press for "turning our entertainment shows into religious crusades." It seems impossible to please the folks on either end of the spectrum.

I'm still looking for Jesus' formula. In the 5th chapter of Luke He was severely criticized by the religious people because He went into the home of Levi, the tax collector, and was the *guest of honor* at a big eating and drinking party that evidently included all kinds of questionable folks—the Bible specifically calls them "notorious sinners."

Jesus' answer to them was, "It is the sick who need a doctor, not those in good health. My purpose is to invite sinners to turn from their sins, not to spend My time with those who think themselves already good enough."

The question I'm always asking is: how was Jesus so truly the Son of God, absolutely sinless and pure, without being a total wet blanket in those tricky, secular situations? The way most of us picture Jesus, He would have walked into a big party where there was drinking, loud music and raucous behavior— and the room would have fallen silent. People would have looked down and begun to edge toward the door. He would have preached a sermon of condemnation, and ordered them to either "shape up or ship out!"

But that's not the way it was! In Matthew 11 Jesus says, "For John the Baptist doesn't even drink wine and often goes without food, and you say, 'he's crazy.' And I, the Messiah, feast and drink, and you complain that I am 'a glutton and a drinking man, and hang around with the worst of sinners.' But brilliant men like you can justify your every inconsistency" (TLB).

Shirley: Didn't He also say not to cast your pearls before swine?

Pat: Yes, He did, and that's a pretty touchy thing to talk about, especially in the 20th century. But I believe He was telling us, "Don't give people more than they're ready to hear. If you try to force-feed deep spiritual truths to people who aren't ready for them, they'll not only reject what you say, but Jesus indicated the swine (spiritually dead people) will turn on you and tear you up!"

We know that we're in a precarious position. We want to share as much of Jesus and His power as we can in any situation, but there are hundreds of millions of people who are not reborn spiritually. They are not even looking for spiritual answers. They don't accept Jesus and the Bible as absolute authority and yet must be reached somehow by somebody with the good news. As I've said to a number of concerned Christian leaders, "If Christian entertainers quit the business and become evangelists, we'll be leaving this gigantic, powerfully influential medium entirely to the devil. And I don't think the Lord wants that."

Shirley: Neither do I—now. One of the most convincing "flags" from the Lord was that woman who saw you in a "Come Together" performance in Lancaster. Remember her?

163

Pat: Yes, she said her daughter dragged her to that purely spiritual occasion, and that she was almost nauseated by it. So much so, in fact, that she got up and left in the middle. She figured we were a bunch of hypocrites, and that this was some sly money-making proposition. She wanted none of it.

Shirley: Then, as she wrote us later, her teenage daughter persuaded her to come to Magic Mountain to see us perform as a family. The woman really didn't want to, but decided she could at least stomach a live entertainment show which obviously couldn't be "religious."

We just did our regular show, entertaining the big crowd, but inserting two or three of our contemporary Jesus songs.

And the woman said, "Something melted inside of me. I realized that your religion wasn't just an act, that you people were real, and *that you had something I wanted!*"

Pat: We didn't even meet the lady that day, but she wrote us that she went home with her daughter, got on her knees and committed her life to the Lord. Since then she has been baptized both in water and the Holy Spirit, and is really moving on with Jesus. We praise the Lord for situations like that!

Shirley: Not just for His power and His willingness to use us—but for being so considerate as to let us know about it. The Lord knew I really needed confirmation at that time that we were doing His will.

I'd love an excuse to get off stage and off camera anyway. It scares me to death! As soon as the Lord lets us know He's through with us, or at least me, as entertainers, I'll say, "Hallelujah!"

Pat: It's good to hear you say that, Honey. I knew back when we made our commitment to the Lord that if we continued to sing and say what we did about Jesus, that whether or not I could survive as a professional entertainer was a big question mark. But when we agreed just a short time ago that we should "bloom where we had been planted," I thanked God. . . . So through flak and flowers, applause and hard knocks, we'll do our best to serve the Lord. As Paul writes, "Let each man remain in that condition in which he was called " (I Corinthians 7:20).

17
Patchwork Paradise

SHIRLEY

Marriage was God's idea. He invented it.

Human history begins with the picture of ideal marriage in the first three chapters of Genesis. We see a perfect marriage, the way God intended it to be. I love the way The Living Bible records it:

Then God said, "Let us make a man, someone like ourselves, to be the master of all life upon the earth and in the skies and in the seas."

So God made man like his Maker.

Like God, did God make man;

Man and maid did He make them.

And God blessed them and told them, "Multiply and fill the earth and subdue it; you are masters of the fish and birds and all the animals. And look! I have given you the seed-bearing plants throughout the earth and all the fruit trees for your food, and I've given all the grass and plants

to the animals and birds for their food."
Then God looked over all that He had made, and it was
excellent in every way. This ended the sixth day.

(Genesis 1:26-31)

So the honeymoon began! I have no idea how long it lasted;
nobody does. Long enough for Adam to name all of the
animals of God's creation, maybe years.

That might have been part of the problem. Who knows?
Maybe Eve got bored. We do know that she wasn't afraid when
the serpent approached her one day.

"Really," he asked? "None of the fruit of the garden?
God says you mustn't eat any of it?"

"Of course, we may eat it," the woman told him. "It's
only the fruit from the tree at the center of the garden that
we're not to eat. God says we mustn't eat it or even touch
it, or we will die."

"That's a lie," the serpent hissed. "You'll not die!"

(Genesis 3:1-4 TLB)

And the conversation went on. You know the story, how the
crafty serpent persuaded the woman to disbelieve the Lord, to
eat the forbidden fruit, and persuade Adam to do the same.
Together they came under the curse of God and were banished
from the garden.

After pronouncing the curse on the serpent, God said to the
woman, "You shall bear children in much pain and suffering,
but even so, you shall welcome your husband's affections, and
he shall be your master" (Genesis 3:16 TLB).

Now I know lots of women don't like the sound of that
today, but that's not some male chauvinist speaking. That's

167

God! He's the one who made us and invented this thing called marriage.

But that's not the whole story.

> "And to Adam," God said, "because you listened to your wife and ate the fruit when I told you not to, I have placed a curse upon the soil. All your life you will struggle to extract a living from it. It will grow thorns and thistles for you, and you shall eat its grasses. All your life, you will sweat to master it until your dying day . . ."
>
> (Genesis 3:17-19 TLB).

It appears painfully clear to me now that man and woman are meant to have problems! Even under ideal conditions, and even if each were perfectly willing to do it God's way, they were going to have trouble! The woman will have pain in child-bearing and child raising. Eternal conflict exists between the sexes, emotional and physical and spiritual. And man is going to have trouble supporting his family, putting food on the table, and wrestling with life in general.

But there is a precious footnote to this promise of tribulation. Genesis 3:21 adds, "And the Lord God clothed Adam and his wife with garments made from skins of animals" (TLB).

Do you realize what this means? Adam and Eve hadn't needed covering before, but with the introduction of guilt and shame and the promise of coming hardship, now they did. And God provided it Himself though it cost the life of innocent creatures.

What an incredible forecast of Jesus' ultimate sacrifice for all of us! And what a powerfully precious demonstration that God would work *with* His fallen creatures, this pitiable duo, the prototype man and wife. He did it then, and He's doing it now.

No matter how rich or poor you may be, no matter how compatible you may be as mates, no matter how many books you read, or whether you start young or late in life, no matter whether you live in peaceful or turbulent times, no matter what—if you want to have a successful marriage, you'll have problems until the day you die. And you'll have to learn to cope with them, or to live with them if you can't find the answers.

Don't expect to get back to the Garden of Eden in your lifetime! No matter who you are, you're going to have rocky times, misunderstandings, disappointments, fights and bleak periods where it seems God has abandoned you. But He hasn't. He's trying to teach you something!

Pat and I have virtually taken off our fig leaves. We've exposed our family problems in the hope that God will use our story to help other married people. When problems mess up your paradise, we want you to know that the Lord is there, ready to cover you and patch things up, if you'll let Him. And afterwards, you'll be stronger than ever!

In the early years Pat and I thought we had it made. We had so much in common. We loved each other. We had children, money, education, a successful career and world acclaim. On top of that, we had the Lord! How could we possibly have trouble?

But trouble came, first in sprinkles, then a downpour, and then a flood. And the soaring divorce statistics tell us that most American families are being lashed around too. Because most of us are woefully ignorant of the Bible, the troubles have taken us by surprise. If we'd only known what to expect (and if we'd known God's will we would have), we'd have kept everything roped down, the sails trimmed, and the cargo and crew safely below deck. But we falsely expected fair weather and clear sailing. It doesn't work that way.

A wonderful Bible teacher once told me the difference between "fork marriages" and "spoon marriages." The computers and marriage counselors often try to create "spoon marriages" in which two people are mated because they have so much in common and fit together like two spoons. But they eventually slide apart, for there's little to hold them together.

God makes "fork marriages." He takes two people and has them face each other like two forks with their points touching. There is tension and resistance. Eventually, though, the points slide between each other and become deeply intertwined. And that's a true marriage!

There's a lot of truth to the old adage, "Opposites attract." Often we women are attracted to qualities in our men that we don't have—and vice versa. That makes for lifelong conflict, but under God, for lifelong growth as well.

It's that way in our marriage to Jesus too. The Lord knew exactly what He was saying when he compared the whole body of believers to Eve, and Jesus to Adam. The home is a laboratory; the family is a workshop where our Creator God is preparing the perfect bride for His Son.

And this bride has sprung from the second Adam's side, just as the first bride did. When that soldier pierced Jesus' side, and blood and water streamed to the ground, a grieving Father God was providing the ultimate covering for you and me. In a sense, for all who will receive it, He was fashioning a bridal gown.

But we can't stay like we are and expect to wear that gown. Bible teacher Bob Mumford gives this beautiful illustration. He was studying the Bible one day, reading that Jesus had gone to prepare eternal mansions for us so that we could live forever with God. Suddenly, the incongruity of it all hit him.

"Lord," he said, "You're perfect and we're so imperfect. You're righteous and we're sinful. When some of my relatives come to visit us, I get fidgety after a few days. Within a week I'm hinting that they should leave. They're my own flesh and blood and I love them, but I don't think I could stand having them in my house for long. How are You going to put up with *us* for eternity?"

And according to Bob the Lord answered, "One of us is going to have to change. And, Son, I don't change."

And that's right! You and I are going to have to change, and the family is one of life's major remodeling shops.

May I share a couple more personal examples?
The other day we were flying home from a performance in
Seattle. I was exhausted and complaining a little to the Lord.
This had been a family singing trip, and I knew in a few days we
were scheduled for still another. Meanwhile, back at home our
schedule held a recording session or two and a photo-interview
by a Swedish film magazine.

"Lord, help Pat to understand how bone-tired I get with all
this activity," I prayed. "He seems to thrive on activity. It even
peps him up somehow; and the more drive he gets, the more
worn out I get."

My eyes were closed, and I was really moaning. I think I
dozed off, still meditating and praying. I had a vision of an
automobile with four wheels, and I understood right away it
had to do with our family traveling together. I saw the left front
tire running like mad and burning up the road. Meanwhile, the
right rear tire had its brakes on! As a result, the whole car
shook like crazy. I knew I was the one who was always putting
on the brakes.

A little later on the same flight I shared this vision with Cherry. She thought about it for a few minutes, and then made this
interesting comment.

"You know, Mom, the Holy Spirit is the axle. You will get
into proper alignment when you let Him show Daddy how you
operate. And at the same time, He'll show you how Daddy
operates. Then maybe you'll stop putting on the brakes, and
Daddy will stop going so fast."

You see why the Holy Spirit is so important in our lives?
After I spoke one time in the Midwest, a lady came up to me.

"I'm a Christian, and have been for a long time. Do I really
need this baptism in the Holy Spirit?" she asked.

"Well," I said, "to me it's like the farmer who has to cultivate
a huge field with a hoe. But as he looks over the vast acreage he
has to cover, he realizes how useless a hoe is for the job. Then a
friend walks by and says he has a tractor and a gang of cultivators which he'll loan the farmer.

"If you were that farmer," I asked the lady, "would you refuse the tractor and cultivators and keep on hacking away with your little hoe?"

She smiled. I believe she got my point.

Many times Jesus compared the kingdom of God to a vineyard. I know now from experience that the Lord wants to cultivate that vineyard and cause growth in every one of us. If we don't cooperate, we're in danger of losing our place in the vineyard!

And cultivation includes pruning. "Every branch that bears fruit, He prunes it, that it may bear more fruit" (John 15:2 NASB).

Ouch! That hurts! Does that mean when we're really bearing fruit, when we apparently have it all together, that the Lord is going to start lopping off parts of us? It surely does.

Why? Because the Lord wants to perfect us, to bring about His kind of holiness in us. The pruning and the problems are necessary so that we can grow straighter and truer and produce more beautiful fruit.

Our first pruning and new growth as a family coincided with the birth of the modern "Jesus movement." Just as hundreds of thousands of young people all over the world were having personal encounters with Jesus, realizing that He is more than a historical figure or a doctrine, we were baptized in the Spirit.

It was wonderful. TV, newspapers and magazines took note of it with some indulgence. We were having Bible studies in our home, baptizing people in our pool, and experiencing great joy in the Lord. It was really a honeymoon for so many of us!

And then the Lord said, "Alright, the honeymoon is over. Now I'm going to cut away some of your dead branches, the parts that can't bear spiritual fruit, and it may hurt. But later on, you'll be glad, because you'll be more productive.

Even though I cringe at times, I'm a candidate for that kind of growth. I want Him to work His holiness in me. So does Pat, and so do our girls and their husbands.

Queen Esther gives us a perfect example. You may

remember that King Ahasuerus was a mighty king who ruled over 127 provinces from India all the way to Ethiopia.

One day he gave a banquet for all of his attendants, the army officers of Persia and Media and the nobles and princes of his provinces. It must have been a fantastic event; it lasted seven days! And while this was going on Queen Vashti, the king's wife, was also giving a banquet for the women in the palace.

Finally, at the climax of the affair King Ahasuerus sent a message to Queen Vashti requesting her to appear with him in her royal crown. She refused!

So King Ahasuerus asked the wise men who were in attendance what he should do. Their advice was that because the queen had wronged not only the king, but also the princes and the people who were present at the banquet, she should be banished. And she was.

To replace Queen Vashti King Ahasuerus sent messengers throughout all his provinces in search of the right girl. Eventually, a young Jewish woman named Esther, whose parents had been taken captive from Jerusalem, was chosen.

At her preparation for the final selection, Esther put herself completely in the hands of Hegai, the king's servant. He was in charge of all the women and responsible for bringing out the best in each of them. And before that she was subjected to a twelve-month preparation period: six months with oil of myrrh and six months with spices.

I did a little research and discovered that myrrh represents a sacrifice of *something that has been crushed in order to bring out its essence to the fullest.* Are you following me? The spices, or sweet savor, during the last six months usually represent *a sacrifice by fire.*

In other words, Esther was willing to submit herself to twelve months of intensive purification in preparation for selection by the king.

Would I have been willing to go through all that, I thought, *and am I willing now to undergo trial in order to be prepared for my King and the blessings He wants me to have?*

Then I remembered how God had said He would supply all of our needs according to His riches in glory. So if I'm willing to allow the purification to go on in me, God will supply whatever grace I need to undergo the treatment.

Esther's willingness, her submission to the king's wishes and to the preparation of Hegai (I believe he's a type of the Holy Spirit today), bore rich fruit. She not only replaced Vashti as queen, but later on she was used by God to save the people of Israel! And she got her own book in the Bible!

If you and I belong to the King, we may never have our own books in the Bible, but our names are written in the Lamb's book of life—and that's enough for me!

There was only one perfect couple, Adam and Eve. But they blew it. They lost their paradise because they were not willing to submit to the King. You and I aren't living in paradise anymore, but if we belong to Jesus, we're living in a kingdom. And the King Himself, by His Holy Spirit, is willing to prune and patch us, to cultivate and educate us, and to transform ragged street urchins into children of the King.

18

Pain Comes
with the Pleasure

SHIRLEY & PAT

Pat: Honey, may I throw a little fire on this chapter?

Shirley: Oh, no! . . . I can tell it's about time to end this book.

Pat: Well, maybe I *am* getting slap-happy. This has been a rugged assignment.

Shirley: Especially for me. I think you find it easier to talk about our failures and trials and triumphs than I do. It *does* hurt to admit your mistakes and to share some of your most intimate moments as a family with people you don't even know. It's difficult for me to do that.

Pat: I told somebody just a couple of days ago, "Shirley and I have been happily married for most of 24 years now. But since we started writing this book together to tell about those years—we've had fourteen fights!"

I was kidding of course, but we have had a number of touchy moments, because we seem to remember things differently. At least the details and the chronology. I know your memory is better than mine, but I just hate to admit it.

Shirley: It's obvious that we've both grown, and working on our story together has been exhilarating and a challenge . . . a sort of painful pleasure.

It would be a great thing for every couple who've been married for at least five years to write their own story, even if it were never published. I'm sure they would see the countless ways that God has helped them through their disappointments and maybe saved them from disaster.

Pat: I agree. But if they do, they had better batten down the hatches because they're in for a storm! It's amazing that two people can live together through the same period of their lives and remember it differently in so many ways.

You know what really puzzled me while we were in the midst of this book? It was so hard to find a quiet time to work together because of the countless interruptions. We changed the phone numbers a couple of times, and *still* it was ringing off the wall. People came to our door unannounced in steady streams. Our household help quit on us three times, and we had an unusual number of skirmishes with illness and emotional flare-ups and breakdowns in communication. Finally you broke down and cried.

"Pat, I can't *take* this anymore. We must be doing something wrong!" you told me.

I mulled that over and then the whole picture became clear.

"No, Honey, we're doing something *right!* I'll bet that's why we're having all this trouble," I said.

Shirley: I got your point immediately. What else should we expect? Here we were, writing a book about the problems married people face, about applying God's principles to those problems, and expecting the Lord Himself to work with us to solve them—and we're surprised that we were having problems ourselves!

It's hard to know whether the Lord or the devil is the source of your current trial. In the magnificent book of Job we find out it was both, in a curious way. Satan asked permission to afflict that good man—and he's the one who brought the disasters, the boils and the accusations—but God permitted it! Eventually all the hardships worked out to Job's great blessing.

Pat: Yes, and it was Paul who said, "No temptation (or test) has overtaken you but such as is common to man; and God is faithful, who will not allow you to be tempted beyond what you are able, but with the temptation will provide a way of escape also, that you may be able to endure it (pass the test)" (I Corinthians 10:13 NASB).

Did we really think that the Lord or the devil would allow us to write a book about principles and problems without putting us to the test again? Good old brother James, author of that book in the New Testament, knew what he was talking about.

"Consider it all joy, my brethren, when you encounter various trials, knowing that the testing of your faith produces endurance. And let endurance have its perfect result, that you may be perfect and complete, lacking in nothing" (James 1:2-4 NASB).

No wonder we were facing every obstacle under the sun while we were trying to write a book about this very principle!

Shirley: Jack Hayford has told us that on Sunday morning, just as he and his family are getting ready for church and his mind is on the four sermons he has to preach—his kids will get into squabbles. He'll discover that he and his wife are at cross-purposes, and everything seems to go wrong at the last minute. Does that sound familiar around your house?

Since that does follow a pattern, maybe there's a reason for it. Psychologists will say that it's the result of tension. But tension itself is an evidence of being out of harmony with God's will. The Bible says, "Be anxious for nothing, but in everything by prayer and supplication with thanksgiving let your requests be made known to God. And the peace of God, which surpasses all comprehension, shall guard your hearts and your minds in Christ Jesus" (Philippians 4:6-7 NASB). I think it goes deeper than tension.

Pat: Sure it does. Why does the Lord say the peace of God shall guard your hearts and minds? Guard against what? In a family situation, in the security of your own home, is there something to guard against? You bet there is!

Especially in your own home you have to be on guard against Satan, the accuser of the brethren, the one who comes "to rob, kill and destroy." He is the enticer who uses our fleshly appetites to corrupt us—the insidious conniver who turns even our good motives and loving concern for each other into dangerous traps (Matthew 16:22-23).

This is important—as important a point as anything in this whole book. As wonderful an institution as the family is, it can also be the place where people are everlastingly warped and doomed. Psychologists tell us that our personalities and characters are shaped very early, and our very attitude toward God can be shaped or twisted by our attitude toward our parents.

There will be a lot of people in hell because their parents hid God from them in their early years. I talk to people all the time who have no concept of a Father God at all, because their own father provided such a poor example. And I'm not blaming the parents totally, because I know Satan is just as near as the Lord and dedicated to thwarting and perverting God's plan for the human race—beginning with the family unit.

Shirley: Pat, I'll bet a lot of people think that we're "going off the deep end" now. But let's take a look at Jesus with His own family around His own table. We call it the Last Supper.

He was surrounded by people He deeply loved and who loved Him too. What could be more peaceful than that? Yet Luke says that Satan had already entered into the heart of Judas, and Jesus softly told the twelve that His betrayer was right there among them.

And just before that He had told His disciples that they would be betrayed by even parents, brothers, relatives and friends, and would be put to death. You can see why it's so important for each member of the family to stay close to Jesus!

Pat: And that's not easy. In fact, the nearer a family wants to be to Jesus, the more severe the tests may be. Follow Jesus on out of the Upper Room and into the Garden of Gethsemane. Out of His family He took the three who were the closest to Him—Peter, James and John—so they could help Him in His greatest trial. Remember His advice to them?

"Keep watching and praying, that you may not enter into temptation; the spirit is willing, but the flesh is weak" (Matthew 26:41 NASB).

What kind of temptation did Jesus expect them to face in the intimacy and quiet of the garden? I think the answer is in verse 43, "And He came back and found them sleeping, for their eyes were heavy."

Some say they were sleepy because of the wine they had drunk, but I think it's more than that. I believe Satan was focusing all his fury and diabolical cunning on that little garden in that crucial hour. And since Jesus had singled them out for a special purpose, Satan was drugging them into sleep, using all his demonic prowess to render them ineffective. We know he can do that! And if he could do it in the garden in the physical presence of Jesus, what can he do in our homes?

Shirley: We know he can work on Christians too. In Acts 5 the Bible says that the devil corrupted Ananias and Sapphira, who were disciples of Jesus! And they appeared to be doing a good thing; they had sold a piece of property and were bringing part of the proceeds to the church. But they kept part of it secretly for themselves. Very "human," wouldn't you say?

> But Peter said, "Ananias, why has Satan filled your heart to lie to the Holy Spirit, and to keep back some of the price of the land? While it remained unsold, did it not remain your own? And after it was sold, was it not under your control? Why is it that you have conceived this deed in your heart? You have not lied to men, but to God." (Acts 5:3,4 NASB)

And the Lord struck them dead on the spot!

My heart breaks when I read this, because I feel that most husbands and wives are capable of the same thing. We all try to do good for our family and other people, but if we deny the Holy Spirit's working and prompting in our lives, we're doomed to failure, or at least only partial success.

Pat: I've always thought the Lord was extremely harsh in this situation. But when I read the results—great fear came upon the whole church, and upon all who heard these things—I believe I see the reason. Marital relationships and the disciples' relationships to each other and to Jesus are important to our Father. He does not want to see them corrupted.

And so, in this early stage of the Church, He took drastic action. And though He may not act so immediately or drastically today, His attitude hasn't changed.

Shirley: It's interesting that Peter asked Sapphira why they had agreed to put the Spirit of the Lord to the *test*? Evidently, the Lord will put up with our blunders and mistakes and ignorance, but when we deliberately resist the work of the Holy Spirit, we're in for real trouble.

Pat: You're on to something, Honey. Paul says in Hebrews 3:7-12 (NASB):

> Therefore, just as the Holy Spirit says, "Today if you hear His voice, do not harden your hearts as when they provoked Me, as in the day of trial in the wilderness, where your fathers tried Me by testing Me, and saw My works for forty years. Therefore I was angry with this generation, and said, 'They always go astray in their heart; and they did not know My ways,' as I swore in My wrath, 'They shall not enter my rest.' "
> Take care, brethren, lest there should be in anyone of you an evil, unbelieving heart, in falling away from the living God.
> But encourage one another day after day.

How did the children of Israel test God? Check it out in Numbers 14. *They refused what God was offering them!* He had prepared a kingdom for them. All they had to do was take it, and they refused.

After the children of Israel had been led out of bondage (saved) and baptized (by the Red Sea and the cloud that hovered over them), "by a miracle God sent them food to eat and water to drink there in the desert; they drank the water that Christ gave them. He was there with them as a mighty rock of spiritual refreshment. Yet after all this most of them did not obey God, and He destroyed them in the wilderness" (I Corinthians 10:3-5 TLB).

Paul says clearly that these things happened to the children of Israel as *examples to us.* What is there for the Christian family then, after they're born again, baptized and faithful to their church?

There is a kingdom to be entered into, full of miracles and the very presence and power of Jesus, the refreshing of the Holy Spirit, and the mighty working of God's plan through each member of the family.

And woe to that family which tests God, refusing to enter into that kingdom. They may seem to get away with it for awhile, but then the roof will cave in! Next comes the long wilderness wandering, as that family is attacked by the temptations of the world and the ravages of demonic enemies.

Shirley: So many *ministers* today are seeing their own homes and marriages break up, and the homes and marriages of their church leaders. Their kids are becoming homosexuals and drug addicts, running away from home and living promiscuously with first one person, then another. And these are the homes of *leaders,* men of God who are supposed to know God's Word! But they resist the power and the gifts of the Holy Spirit, for doctrinal reasons or whatever, and then wonder why their family is coming apart.

Pat: I know personally of one church where the leaders took a strong public stand against the direct operation of the Holy Spirit. In less than two years one elder's son was killed; another's daughter was raped; another's son acknowledged he was a homosexual; another's son died of cancer; another's marriage broke up. And on it went.

Please understand me; I don't believe God did that to those good men and their families. But I do believe they walked away from God's protection and became "sitting ducks" for that ravenous beast, that roaring lion whom Peter identifies as Satan. God protects those who do His will.

Shirley: Remember the young entertainer and his equally talented wife who prayed with us recently? They loved each other so much, but they were having marital problems and realized they needed the Lord.

So we prayed with them, and each made a commitment to Jesus. But soon after that, and after they had become regular church-goers, they were divorced.

Eventually, the religious writer for the *Los Angeles Times* called Pat and asked him his reaction, since it had become known that the couple had prayed with us and been to our Bible studies.

"Yes, I believe that entertainer and his wife have both made real commitments to the Lord," Pat told the writer. "I believe they love each other and their kids, and that God still wants them together as man and wife. But they're always traveling, sometimes in different directions, and have not continued in constant Christian fellowship. So the devil has shot them down.

"Shirley and I intend to keep on praying for them, hoping they'll see how desperately they need the fulness of the Holy Spirit and individual submission to His will in their lives. If that happens, I believe God can bring them back together."

And, oh, I pray that's what happens. We love those two so much.

Pat: That episode convinced us more than ever that we needed to write this book, for whatever good it can do for families. We've seen that it's not enough to just introduce people to Jesus, baptize them, dry them off and send them on their way. They may have a brief spiritual honeymoon, but then all hell will break loose!

Oh, I know Satan may appear to leave some couples alone even if they're not committed to Jesus. There are always examples of couples and families who seem to be just fine, without any kind of commitment to the Lord at all. But it's easy to see through the devil's tactics.

If you were the devil, wouldn't you let a few people "get away with it" for almost their whole lives, in order to trick countless others into a false sense of security, into the same aimless existence? Many times in the Bible God warns that this will happen, and that the righteous should never envy the apparent prosperity of the wicked.

I'm thinking of an extremely successful movie producer, who seems to break all the spiritual rules, and gets richer and more successful all the time. He's at the top of the heap, makes tremendously important films, has the jet set crowd in his home continuously, and lives in splendor without any visible regard for God or the Bible or spiritual reality.

I used to wonder how that could be. Then recently, I learned that this man's only son had jumped from a building in New York City and dashed himself and his father's future hopes on the sidewalk below.

His father was almost as shattered as his son. He kept asking himself and his friends, "Why? Why did he do it? He wasn't on drugs. He was grown and in business, with everything to live for. He could have had everything I own. Why would he do this to himself?"

Shirley: As tragic as this situation is, the answer is simple. Without God's principles, the problems of life will eventually destroy us.

As mothers and wives we must follow God's order:

> You wives must submit to your husbands' leadership in the same way you submit to the Lord. For a husband is in charge of his wife in the same way Christ is in charge of His body the church. (He gave His very life to take care of it and be its Savior!) So you wives must willingly obey your husbands in everything, just as the church obeys Christ.
>
> (Ephesians 5:22-24 TLB)

Pat: And I echo the words of Paul in the next several verses:

> And you husbands, show the same kind of love to your wives as Christ showed to the church when He died for her, to make her holy and clean, washed by baptism and God's Word; so that He could give her to Himself as a glorious church without a single spot or wrinkle or any other blemish, being holy and without a single fault.
> That is how husbands should treat their wives, loving them as parts of themselves. For since a man and his wife are now one, a man is really doing himself a favor and loving himself when he loves his wife! No one hates his own body but lovingly cares for it, just as Christ cared for His body the church, of which we are parts.
>
>   (Ephesians 5:25-30 TLB)

And now you know the full reason for the title of this book. In a human marriage and in our spiritual marriage to Jesus, we can count on a brief honeymoon where everything seems to be easy, but after that we can expect problems which can only be overcome by applying God's principles. He gives us the formula for success in His Word. You'll never find it anywhere else.

Mr. And Mrs. A. A. Boone, Pat's parents, read the document which "de-fellowshipped" them from their church. The church took this action after the Boones came into a new experience with the Holy Spirit.

(Left to right) Laury, Doug (Lindy's husband), Lindy, Shirley, Pat, Cherry, Dan (Cherry's husband), Debby.

JoAnn (Phlug) and Chuck Woolery asked Shirley and Pat to be godparents when their baby was born.

(Above) Andrae Crouch and Pat team up for an Easter special for British television.

(Left) The proud father readies his camera at Debby's graduation.

(Below) On a tour to Israel George Otis (right), Pat, and Dan O'Neill (Pat's son-in-law) met with then Prime Minister Yitzhak Rabin (left).

A beaming Pat and Shirley watch daughter Cherry become the bride of Dan O'Neill.

nteen

STALGIA
OM

TY NEW
OTHES
OM
E 40s
50s
60s

Y HOLLYWOOD'S
JCK IN THE
OD OLD DAYS"

ercise bugs you
NCE AWAY YOUR FLAB

CK TO SCHOOL?
CK A SKILLET

N LOVE
FOREVER?

UNG AMERICA TODAY:
wing Up in a Broken Home

VAYS TO
NTROL YOUR ANGER

W A KISS MADE
QUIT SMOKING"

VING SOLO
h a girl pilot, age 17

Pat Boone
and his daughter
Debby, 17